Dedicated to

The women and men who respond to
the call to serve God's people
in Zambia, Africa.

Trasna

The pilgrims paused on the ancient stones

In the mountain gap.

Behind them stretched the roadway they had traveled.

Ahead, mist hid the track.

Unspoken the question hovered:

Why go on? Is life not short enough?

Why venture further on strange paths, risking it all?

Surely that is a gamble for fools...or lovers.

Why not return quietly by the known road?

Why be a pilgrim still?

A voice they knew called to them, saying

this is Trasna, the crossing place.

Choose! Go back if you must.

You will find your way easily by yesterday's fires.

There may be life in the embers yet.

If that is not your deep desire,

Stand still, lay down your load.

Take your life firmly in your two hands,

(Gently...you are trusted with something precious)

while you search your heart's yearnings:

What am I seeking? What is my quest?

When your star rises deep within,

Trust yourself to its leading.

You will have light for your first steps.

This is Trasna, the crossing place.

Choose!

This is Trasna, the crossing place.

Come!

Poem by Sister Raphael Cortsdine, PBVM
Published by The Presentation Sisters of Victoria, Australia
In book entitled Songs of the Journey
Permission to use granted by
Sister Maria Lazzaro, PBVM
Congregation Leader
Presentation Sisters Victoria

Trasna

❧❧❧

By

Sister Margie Hosch, OSF,
Sister Connie Fahey, FSM
Mary Catherine Harris
Bill Hancock

Trasna
Copyright © 2018
Bill Hancock

ISBN 978-1-941069-82-0

Prose Press Pawleys Island SC 29585
prosencons@live.com

Thanks to the co-authors of this book: Sister Margie Hosch, OSF, Sister Connie Fahey, FSM and Mary Catherine Harris, for freely revealing their inspiring, heartfelt and intense stories.

Special thanks to Bob O'Brien, Christina Cauvcci, Rosemary Galvin and Lori Hancock for their help and insight.

The material in this book reveals the words, thoughts
and adventures of three women who
have lived life changing episodes as the result of
experiencing and pursuing individual
Trasna moments.

Cover Photo by
Sister Margie Hosch, OSF

Table of Contents

Chapter One

Trasna, The Journey
...Ahead, the track to be traveled

The 10 o'clock Mass at Our Lady Star of the Sea in North Myrtle Beach, S.C. has just ended. Sister Margie Hosch, OSF, is standing near the altar speaking with two parishioners about her presentation during Mass in which she described the needs of the poor in Zambia. Another parishioner walks up and stands, waiting for Sister Margie to finish speaking. He has listened to the Sister's presentation and realized that there is much more to her story than She has been able to convey. He thinks, "She has tried to put twenty-five pounds in a five-pound bag!" As a result he decides to offer writing Sister Margie's story. Now while waiting he has second thoughts, "Why not return quietly by the known road?" Sister Margie finishes talking and turns toward him. A Trasna Moment! He says, "Sister, I'm a published author and I would like to write your story."

She replies, "Oh! How wonderful! What is your name? And give me a hug!"

And so it begins:

Early Years:

Sister Margie was the fifth child of eight born to Margaret

(Weber) Hosch and her husband Al Hosch. The Hosch's first child, Albert, died at birth. Their following children were Marilyn, Ruth, Joan, Allan, Margie, David, Ann and Steve.

Margaret was a teacher in a one-room school house before her marriage to Al. After their marriage they owned and operated a dairy farm near Cascade, Iowa. As they grew up, their children all helped with the farm chores, including herding the cows while riding their Shetland pony named Spot, plowing fields using a tractor, feeding chickens and gathering eggs. As a general rule the older siblings cared for the younger ones.

Margie remembers:

When I was small, before electricty, Dad would go into Cascade every Wednesday and Saturday night to play cards with his friends. When he came home, he would bring ice cream, and woke us up to eat it before it melted. I remember asking the next morning, "Did we eat ice cream last night?"

Some evenings Mom would dress us up for bed in our best pajamas. Then we would go to town (Cascade) and whoever had the nicest pajamas would go in to buy the ice cream cones.

On Sunday afternoons we went fishing with Dad; went for rides through the country and stopped for ice cream cones; or went to visit relatives or had them visit us. Many evenings we played cards, either Euchre, Canasta or 500. Popcorn was our favorite snack. Dad made it with butter and sugar. Only Joan developed his knack for making sugar popcorn.

Dad had a great sense of humor. I remember when the assistant pastor, Father Gregory Hemesath, would come down the lane to have a rendezvous with Dad to see who could tell the funniest stories and jokes. He would come in and dust off our Bible, which Mom had already dusted as soon as she saw him driving down the lane. We gathered in the living room for the funniest show in the countryside. We laughed and laughed with each joke and story being better than the one before. This happened about every other month.

At Dad's funeral, the priest started his homily saying, "There is no carbon copy of Al Hosch; he was unique and special." One evening, before he passed, he was sitting in his big lounge chair and uttered his thoughts, "It won't be so bad to die if everyone wouldn't feel so bad about it." I responded, "But Dad, that is the price we all pay for loving you so much."

Faith for me was caught more than taught. My mother kept us on the pathway to Jesus, Mary and Joseph. Every evening, regardless of rain, snow, sleet, hail or exhaustion from seasonal work in the fields, feeding chickens, or milking cows, we would hear her invitation, "Will someone please pass out the rosaries!" Sometimes her request was followed with a chorus of, "Not tonight, Mom, we are too tired." Dad was the most exhausted but never raised a discouraging word and led us all in getting on our knees to pray. Often, towards the end of the rosary we were serenaded by snores coming from our Dad. Prayers and snoring were heard many a night with no complaints coming from anyone. Then Mom would remind us to say three Hail Marys before falling to sleep so that we would know how to answer the call to follow when we grew up.

I learned a huge lesson from Dad about faith. After a devastating hail storm totally destroyed our whole corn crop, I watched him walk the stripped corn fields back and forth for the entire day. I couldn't help but wonder how he was feeling and what he would say about our God who loves us so much. At supper that night we waited for Dad to speak. He said, "God spoke to me while I walked those fields of stripped corn and told me there is something more important to the Hosch family than Iowa corn."

Mom never let us complain about the behavior of another person. One night I thought I really had a righteous complaint and conveyed it to Mom. Her answer to me was, "Margie, you never know what that person is experiencing in their family or with other people." I have never forgotten her gentle lesson.

I can describe my mother as bright, gentle, kind, wise, hard working, deeply religious, close with her six sisters and very intuitive in noticing when someone needed some extra attention. What a gift she was for all of us.

My dad was very intelligent, artistic, creative, had a great sense of humor, and very hard-working. He always let me go to the movies every Wednesday and Saturday nights. He came to my basketball games and I always looked for him in the bleachers.

As for basketball, I was thrilled to be on the team. Dad had our hired man put up a basketball hoop in the orchard so we could practice our shots. My moment of glory happened one evening when we were playing the Holy Cross team. The ceiling in the gymnasium was very low. It was my night to shine. On one of my shots I sent the ball up to the ceiling where it hit and went down into the basket. I ended up with 32 points that night.

Dancing became the delight of my high school days. On Thursday nights a band would come to play at our Knights of Columbus Hall in Cascade. We didn't have to have a date. Most of my class gathered around the edges of the floor and waited for someone to ask us to dance. If a boy didn't ask someone to dance we would dance with each other. It wasn't unusual to find girls dancing together to learn the new dances. Girls were better dancers than boys. So, we would teach the steps to our classmates. We just had a ball.

I would come to the dance with my brother, Allan. Because he was dating someone he would ask me to find a way home. However, he watched to see that I was going with the right people. One time he told me not to go with a certain person again. I felt he really cared about me. He was so solicitous that his sister was protected and would come to no harm.

When we became high school seniors, we branched out to the larger ballrooms in Cedar Rapids and Dubuque. We needed a date to go that far from Cascade. I was so proud of how the older married couples there accepted our presence at these dances. They would come and dance with us and sometimes show us some new dance steps.

My brother David was two years younger than me. He was going to his first dance. Mom asked me to teach David some basic steps. At first I teased him but after seeing my Mother's look of disapproval, I took it seriously. David became a good dancer.

Growing up gave us many opportunities to play with our neighbors who lived within a radius of a mile from us. For Christmas we received family presents like a bike, ice skates, skis, and sleds. We had lots of Sunday afternoons coming together to enjoy the winter's snow on the hills it covered. In the summer we met at the swimming pool or played softball in our orchard.

How did all those three Hail Marys work for me while growing up? Well, I was on the road to marrying some one I loved very much. However, I was restless when looking down the pathway of my life. My sister Joan had entered the Sisters of Saint Francis four years previous to my graduating from high school. Deep within me, I just wanted to tell people more about Jesus. My family experiences had planted the seed to believe in a God whose love outlasts all evil, hatred, personal weaknesses and sin. I will never forget the moment I made my decision to join the Sisters of Saint Francis and leave marriage behind. I was washing the separator disks that separate the cream from milk. A flash of surrender came upon me and I knew that joining the Sisters of Saint Francis, a community of women, who all share the same passion for the Gospel while living in community around the world, was my calling. Those three Hail Marys said over and over for years gave me the grace to say, "I will follow you , Jesus!" (Trasna moment!)

During my first three years at Mount St. Francis I remember one recurring longing. Through my bedroom window I could often hear music being played at the Melody Mill Dance Hall in Dubuque. This may seem strange but dancing was one of the most difficult things for me to give up when I joined the Sisters of St. Francis. Oh, how I love Jesus, was said over and over to myself during those days.

The Climb:

Margie completed a degree in Elementary Education at Briar Cliff University run by the Franciscans in Sioux City and successfully completed her religious formation. She took her final vows in 1958 with the Sisters of St. Francis of the Holy Family in Dubuque.

Sister Margie started her teaching career with assignments in the suburbs of Chicago, Minneapolis and rural Iowa. She continued her studies at the University of Detroit for a Master's in Religious

Education, conducted workshops and began to write. She co-authored a Holy Family Program for parents to be the primary teachers of their children. Parents, six couples per group, met to learn their faith as adults. They were given guides to prepare their children for receiving the sacraments of Reconciliation and Eucharist. The program was examined by the Diocesan Office in Minneapolis and eventually adopted by the diocese. Other dioceses followed in making the approach an optional technique for preparing children for the sacraments.

Sister Margie became aware of the needs of her students and their families wherever she went. She realized that there was a need for a holistic approach in addressing student problems and that frequently the problems were within the family. During her summers she continued going to school and received a Master's in Counseling from St. Mary's University in Winona, MN. She then qualified as a Certified Marriage and Family Consultant. Then Sister Margie teamed up with Sister Dorothy Heiderscheidt, who was counseling Sisters in Dubuque, Iowa. They created and designed the Wholeness/Holiness Retreat which was given for Sisters during the summers.

Based on her strong educational base and ability to bring a Catholic Christian perspective to her teaching and family skills, she was called to be Diocesan Director of Religious Education for the Springfield, Cape Girardeau Diocese in Missouri. Soon after, she was elected as Interstate Regional Coordinator of her religious community, Sisters of St. Francis in Dubuque, IA.

After serving in these administrative tasks for eight years she was eager to return to direct ministry in the field. She left the administrative assignments to become a Marriage and Family

Therapist in Kansas City to assist people out of adversity. She worked with those who were overcome with poverty, grief, pain, loss and depression. She did her best to do as Jesus did, by bringing hope, peace and healing to those in need.

In 1992, a colleague told Sister Margie about a need in South Carolina for which she was well-suited. She interviewed and became a Marriage and Family Therapist at Prince of Peace Parish in Taylors, SC. There she started programs dealing with structured marriage preparation, interpersonal problem-solving and communications improvement to provide support for the divorced and separated, as well as their children. She also initiated a companion ministry to support those who were experiencing sickness, suffering or the loss of a loved one. As an extra, while she was there, for six months the Prince of Peace Parish was without a priest, so Sister Margie served as Pastoral Administrator.

In 1996 she again felt the call to minister more directly to the needs of the poor so she accepted the position as Coodinator of Catholic Charities for the Piedmont Deanery. Sister Margie stayed for eleven years at Catholic Charities. Each day started with a prayer for the disenfranchised and those in need. Then she went to work enlisting volunteers and donors, establishing collaborative efforts with secular and other religious agencies in the region. Her areas of concern and action were: families needing financial assistance, counseling assistance, food for sustenance and emotional support, support and assistance to immigrants, a focused support for grandparents raising their grandchildren, employment support, dental service for those unable to afford it, community activism for peace, justice and racial equality and development of collaboration between people along with agencies to serve the needs of the disadvantaged.

In 2002 it became necessary for the Catholic Charities organization to find new quarters to operate from because their working space at Greenville's St. Mary Church was needed by the church due to a remodeling effort. Sister Margie went to work and coodinated an effort to build the Gallivan Center on the St. Anthony of Padua site, on Greenville's West Side. This new facility would provide space for Catholic Charities, St. Anthony Church administration, community ministries of Bon Secours and Mercy Housing. The new center's location put it at the heart of a low income area with a large African American population. While the new center was in process, Catholic Charities moved into temporary space provided at no cost by two Greenville attorneys.

Bishop Robert J. Baker blessed the Gallivan Center site minutes after lightning flashed, thunder rumbled and rain fell. Sister Margie stood with the more than one hundred guests outside the building, looked up at the clearing sky and said, "God has already blessed this site!"

Good works continued on at Catholic Charities and Sister Margie completed eleven years with the organization, along with fifty years of her ministry.

Chapter Two
Why Continue to Be a Pilgrim?
...Why venture further on strange paths, risking all?

Sister Margie reached a point in her ministry where many of her associates retire from their working lives. She decided that rather than retire she would begin to minister to women in need. During her years of service she had become aware of the plight of many women in society and women in the church. She had had numerous contacts with victims of abuse, discrimination, insecurity and women who were left to maintain families and households on their own. Also, she had encountered capable women with potential who had not been permitted or encouraged to utilize their God-given ability.

Considering this experience, Sister Margie decided to provide the Wholeness/Holiness Retreats for Women with the objective of, "Opening Minds and Hearts to the Loving Embrace of God." (Trasna moment!)

A Wholeness/Holiness Retreat for Women is a seven-day intensive retreat designed to integrate the spiritual and psychological aspects of a woman's life. Multiple strategies are utilized to help each woman develop a new sense of inner-strength and self-nurturing.

Each woman processes through daily individual and group spiritual direction, counseling, prayer and creative expression sessions. An in-depth wellness and opening of the mind and heart is promoted. A safe, holy environment is provided for women who have come to a turning point in their lives and desire greater wholeness.

The retreats aim at enhancing a feminine spirituality through encountering the foot prints of our loving God in creation, contemplation, centering prayer, Scripture, poetry, movement, song, journaling, stories, art expression, imagery, nature walks, drumming, Labyrinth and Cosmic walks. The retreats last for seven days and are limited to seven participants per session.

New Associate – Beginning of a Spiritual Partnership:
Sister Margie's Perspective:

I was giving a Wholeness/Holiness Retreat to a group of Sisters in the southern part of South Carolina when I first met Sister Connie Fahey who was attending the Retreat. She was in the process of completing her great work as the founder of Hospice in Horry County, SC. I admired her dedication to the sick and dying, her administrative aptitude and gentle spirit. A member of the Franciscan Sisters of Mary from St. Louis, Missouri, she followed the Lord's call to minister in a variety of health care ministries. She received a bachelor's degree in medical technology and advanced degrees in administration, education and spiritual direction and ministered in Health Care Systems. She established a hospice home care program, established school of medical technology in South Carolina and served on the Franciscan Sisters of Mary congregation's leadership team. At this point she was ministering as a spiritual director and volunteering.

Since Sister Connie was finishing her work with Hospice, I cast my line to her and invited her to team with me to give retreats. To my delight and amazement she said, "Yes!" After that she attended a course in Spiritual Direction and took on that role during the retreats.

She was a brilliant master at drawing the sisters and lay women into using poetry, song, music, movement and the arts into their relationship with God and all creation. Being from a Franciscan Religious Community, she kept me in touch with reality by using her sensate abilities, because I am an "off the scale" intuitive. As a result, we made a good team. She was a great companion and always a gift to me giving Wholeness/Holiness Retreats over the next five years.

During a retreat I was giving by myself, one of the Sisters at that retreat was Sister Bella Vethemuthu from Lusaka, Zambia. After the retreat, Sister Bella asked if I would consider coming to Lusaka to give the retreat to the religious sisters in the Lusaka Diocese.

I was thrilled by the idea but realized that the mission would be overwelming for one person and that I would need a partner. I told Sister Bella a partner was needed and she agreed.

I immediately called my friend and associate Sister Connie Fahey, FSM who had been working side by side with me. Sister Connie was back in Wisconsin. I asked her if she would be willing to team with me in Zambia. Much to my delight, she said, "Yes!" (Trasna moment!)

Sister Connie Fahey's Perspective:

Going to Zambia with my friend Sister Margie was an opportunity to share a lifetime of experiences and learnings. It was a conscious choice to share my personhood and to imbibe how other human beings of a vastly different culture celebrate and ritualize their lives and understanding of the Mystery we call God. My life was and is about being a loving, compassionate woman, no matter where I worked. My calling from my youth until today is about being accepting and learning from diverse religious and belief systems. And maybe most importantly, being immersed in another's world is about being changed, seeing with eyes of my heart and being challenged to remove blinders and begin to understand what it means, as St. Paul says, "to put on the mind of Christ."

I know what it feels like to be the eldest child of eleven siblings and being awe-struck with the beauty of each new-born baby as it entered our house in Madison, Wisconsin. I have hundreds of memories about working in a pediatric hospital where many families courageously faced life-threatening illnesses and many children succumbed to death in St. Louis, Missouri. I have experienced the joy of growing in intellectual knowledge through obtaining various degrees from reputable universities.

In my professional life, I spent years of peering through a microscope and seeing cells and chromosomes in body fluids and blood, wondering about life's mysteries. I spent many years of being a manager and administrator of organizations, departments and entities needing this kind of expertise.

Also, I can tell you how it feels to be selected by your peers to be a spiritual and canonical leader of a congregation of women religious who heroically and quietly give their lives to provide hands-on health care, health education and who built with bricks and mortar the buildings that serve many towns and cities of four states.

I enjoyed being in the midst of systemic changes of my

FSM congregation and health care system when they began an evolutionary process of unifying two congregations and health care systems by renaming the congregation and setting the health care ministry on a new path. This has resulted in the transfer of power from the sisters to dedicated lay persons.

After my corporate leadership ended, I became engaged in a Hospice ministry in South Carolina. It was a wonderful experience to be accepted by people who talk funny and have cultural mores that aren't like those of the Midwest. But even more importantly, this ministry gave me insight about what is important as I live one, precious life to cherish the beauty and sufferings of my life's journey. The Hospice ministry is about living and being fully alive even as one's body prepares to let go of the breath that inspirits every human being.

Death is a reality that happens to every inch of the cosmos created by Holy Incomprehensible Mystery. It doesn't matter what others believe about life after death if one knows they are part of the universe's patterns and rhythms. What will be, will be. All you need to do is prepare yourself to be the person your Creator created you to be. Then all will be well not only in this life but in whatever kind of life happens after the dust settles.

Being immersed in family, friends' and strangers' dying processes, mourning and grieving loved ones' deaths while creating a sacred space for this seminal human event caused me to reflect. "What does it mean to be human?" To be conscious of the fact that we humans are like one boson in a cosmic reality so huge and beyond our knowing that I want to share my God-given gifts with others so that they may come to a deep awareness and understanding of who they are as God's work of art.

Chapter Three

This Is Trasna, the Crossing Place
...Surely that is a gamble for fools...or lovers

Preparing for the trip – Sister Margie:

I remember how much pride I had for Sister Connie Fahey, she never hesitated to say, "Yes!" She was a healthy sensate who steered me, a full-grown intuitive, around the details that this mission trip called for. The preparations required getting funding, vaccinations, medicines we needed to take in case of sickness, flight planning and obtaining Visas. We also had to contact the Presentation Sisters in Lusaka to set the trip date and schedule three, one-week-long retreats, each at a different place for eight sisters per retreat.

Thinking about the magnitude of this undertaking, I had concerns about what we were about to do so I kept thinking, "I can do this; Jesus knows my limitations." As good fortune would have it, before leaving for Zambia I attended a gathering of the Sisters of St. Francis in Dubuque, Iowa. During one of the presentations a demonstration was given by Sister Judy on how to move out fears and negative thoughts and take on positive renewed energy to do good. During one of our breaks, we were asked to tend to our lives and move out any negative energy which inhibits our positive energy for good.

So, I took a walk to the cemetery where our deceased sisters are buried. Upon gathering their spirit of serving and following the footsteps of Jesus, I bent toward their spirit with my arms outstretched before them and threw away my fears and reservations. Then, with my outstretched arms, I gathered their spirit toward me to send me on my way to Zambia the next week. As I did this, I was seized with empowerment so forceful I had to take several steps backward to find my balance. (Trasna moment!)

I lived within their presence, gathered within me from this event, feeling strengthened and ready to meet all adversity with little fear. I was companioned by the sister spirits who had gone before me. "Fear not," says Jesus and the sisters who are now gathered within me. I was feeling graced by a presence so strong that I trusted more in my capability to make a difference in the lives of the sisters we were to companion.

It was a challenge packing a suitcase, with very little information on weather and housing. We knew we would be arriving towards the end of the rainy season. I wondered how I would fight the mosquitoes, spiders, other unknown insects. This phobia for bugs and insects was something I knew I was going to have to manage every day.

Another concern was, would our spirits meet? Would the retreats feed their souls? Will our differences in culture and languages come together in deepening our call to follow Jesus by focusing on the poor? Would I be an instrument of grace for each sister, and would our cultural differences blend to discover how much we all are loved and held sacred by each other, by those who have gone before us and by our loving God?

Of course, the biggest concern was the aspect of illness from malaria and unknown diseases. The medicines and treatments would not be able to rid us of the many unknown diseases. However, these fears will not stop our mission. We would be an instrument of God's love and peace. I would receive the necessary grace to accomplish this mission. Thank you, my God, and my sisters who are dwelling in the mansion of many rooms.

Zambia, 2009 – Sister Connie:

How does one measure the cavernous depths of love of one person for another? Is it possible to make an estimation of the magnitude of pain that a human's heart can bear? What happens when a person's sea of pain touches the shores of another human's compassion? Can the unrelenting and all-encompassing poverty of a society be pierced through by the magnanimity of a few valiant women?

I didn't know these were my questions as I entered the airport in Lusaka, Zambia at daybreak and was singled out by a pudgy, grinning priest to be escorted through the maze of the country's bureaucracy. I had no idea that by the end of thirty days immersed in the lives of women from India, Ireland, Zambia, the Congo, Zimbabwe, Micronesia, Mexico and Italy that I would grieve leaving them behind as I returned to my home in the United States.

What are the words which could possibly describe the magnificence and splendor of the Victoria Falls and then contrast that glorious spectacle with the stories of survival and heroism told by God's faithful women laboring at the boundaries of lucidity to serve the impoverished?

One reads in the guide books that Zambia has a population of 11.5 million, with 40 percent of the people living in urban areas. Statistics indicate that the infant mortality rate is around 10 percent, while the average life expectancy for a Zambian is 38.4 years. That equates to the life expectancy of 37 years around 1850 in the United States just before the Civil War.

In Zambia, a great majority of the people live in poverty, with an unemployment rate at 80 percent. Forty-six percent of the population is under fifteen years of age. It is estimated that about 20 percent of the population between the ages of 15 and 49 are infected with AIDS. Women religious from around the world are serving those sick and dying of AIDS and the orphans created by the disease. In Lusaka alone, there are five thousand orphans being cared for by committed and dedicated women and men. However, the statistics tell nothing of the warmth, kindness and beauty of the Zambian people.

After a couple of days of adjusting to the time change and

being welcomed into the country by the wonderful hospitality of the Presentation Sisters, we held our first retreat at a Franciscan Seminary outside of Lusaka. We went to Mass at the seminary and experienced powerful singing by the brothers and priests.

The Retreat Center had many lemon and grapefruit trees, banana plants and a working farm. So there was plenty to eat and space to walk around and enjoy the atmosphere. Each night we gazed at the full moon and the brighter than bright African sky, filled with millions upon millions of stars.

After the retreat we traveled to Kizitos, three hours south of Lusaka, to a remote village where the Monze Diocese has a Pastoral Center. We traveled on dirt roads full of pot holes to get there. The center is run by the Handmaids of BVM, an indigenous community. It seems that each bishop has an indigenous group of Zambian Sisters working in his diocese.

We were settled into separate houses. There were twenty two-bedroom houses on the property along with a church, eating hall, and meeting places. Again we experienced a wonderful choir each morning as the sisters sang their Tonga hymns and danced to a rhythm beat on drums.

The retreat was quite powerful as the sisters dealt with their issues; some were quite unique, but most were the same as those of sisters in the USA. At night, we were warned to stay in our house because the dogs are let loose at 10 pm to keep the property secure. So, we heard dogs howling and barking all night everywhere in Zambia, keeping watch over the humans. Zambians are worried about their safety, so we took all the precautions they told us to take.

From Kizitos, we went to Livingstone for a three-day respite. On the way, we stopped in Monze and toured the Holy Sisters' Hospital. The hospital is comprised of a dozen one-story brick white painted buildings. The men's and women's wards were in large buildings that had seventy beds with mattresses down the middle aisle for patient overflow. Both wards were full with medical patients on one side and surgical patients on the other; there was one nurse per ward. One family member was allowed to care for each patient. Everything was clean, although the hospital beds were older than anything I've seen with steel frames and hand cranks to adjust them.

The pediatric building was full of sick babies. There was a separate building for babies with AIDS. The delivery department had about thirty mothers and newborns. Mother and child would stay for 24 hours and then be discharged. Women in labor were sitting outside in the courtyard on a wall waiting to be brought into the delivery ward. There was a separate ICU and surgical building. All bookkeeping was kept in large ledger books.

The pharmacy was neat and clean and the storeroom was typical of any pharmacy. However, the previous week they didn't

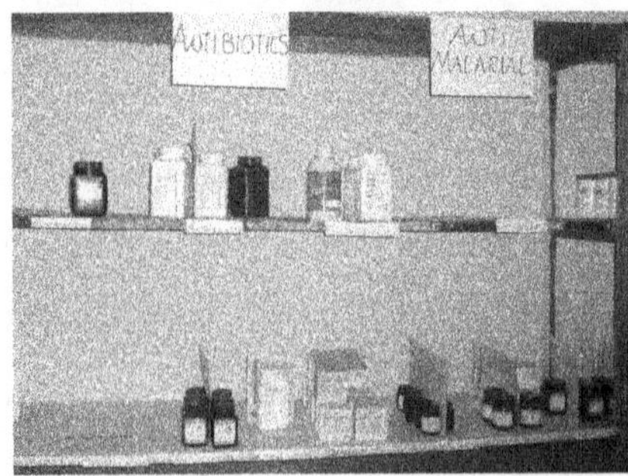

have anything to dispense. Evidently, the money ran out and they couldn't order drugs for a week. About a fourth of the budget is supposed to come from the government but is not dependable because healthcare money often runs out or is siphoned off for other programs. The rest of the budget comes from fees charged but not necessarily collected.

One of the hardest situations facing the country is the HIV epidemic. There are many reasons for this epidemic, but most of it is due to sexual promiscuity. Tribal mores accept polygamy and many men have several wives and continue spreading the disease. They leave a woman with five, six or seven children and no means of income and go on to the next woman. It is almost incomprehensible how the women are used and abused.

The Zambian women are very strong, but the tribal culture and the witchcraft that goes along with tribal beliefs are a huge challenge for them. The sisters establish farms, set up small communes of eight to ten houses for vulnerable women and their children. There, they teach marketable skills to both the women and the orphans.

The women religious in Zambia are not only pioneers but are valiant, holy women who navigate the systems and culture which subjugate Zambian women and children to life-long poverty. The European religious are doing everything in their power to turn over the many projects they have initiated to the indigenous women religious congregations as quickly as possible. These white-haired European sisters are aware that there are no young European sisters to follow them.

Resuming the trip to Livingston, we traveled on dusty two-way highways with the ever-present potholes in the roadway. The trip was not very scenic because it was much like going through a dust storm. Once in a while the wind blew in our favor so we could see ahead as we moved to and fro to avoid the potholes. Eventually, we got to Livingstone, which is a fair-sized tourist town. Everyone visits there to see Victoria Falls, as we also did. What a sight! It was half full so we didn't get drenched by the Falls spray. The Zambezi River flows into the Falls, which really is about a dozen falls all going over banks cascading down into the gorge below. We were met by baboons at the rails overlooking the Falls. The park officials warned us to be careful because the baboons are afraid of people wearing slacks like us. Later in the day, we sat on a deck overlooking the Zambezi River and watched the hippos and crocodiles.

We visited with the Franciscans who run a hospice in Livingstone. They serve three thousand clients in their homes. Most have HIV. The sisters do not receive salaries. The Irish sisters receive some monies for their living expenses through the Irish government, but the others who do social services are dependent upon grants and donations. Zambian sisters can work in government institutions and receive a small salary, but non-Zambians cannot be employed by institutions, hospitals or schools. So the sisters are always looking for funding. The Catholic Relief Services has helped the Hospice financially, as well as other International groups.

When I walked into the meeting room at the Hospice, I saw that they had a large bulletin board with the Vision, Mission, Goals and Objectives just like at Mercy Hospice in Horry County, South Carolina. These Irish sisters know how to run an organization.

From the Hospice, we went to another of the Presentation Sisters' ministries, a youth center. It is a series of buildings, much like our technical colleges, which educates orphans and other needy youth in occupations such as plumbing, carpentry, food services, tailoring and computer technology. From the Youth Center we went to Olga's restaurant, a business run by Youth Center graduates. There we had pizza and a Zambian beer. The restaurant is a source of income for the Youth Center. The meal was served in fine fashion and the young people running the business are quite professional.

After our meal, we went to the Livingstone Museum which contains a vast amount of information on and history of the many Zambian tribes, governance of Zambia and the impacts of colonization. That evening we took a sunset trip down the Zambezi River. The boat maneuvered around hippos and elephants crossing the river, while we enjoyed the spectacular sunset.

After our few days of respite, we went back into the car to make the dusty trip back to Lusaka. Along the way we stopped at a Presentation Convent for lunch. We toured their ministry site which consisted of two communal housing compounds for widows left homeless because of AIDS. The sisters have developed housing in each compound consisting of eight houses with four rooms in each house and a water supply in each compound's middle so that all can use it. Water is a luxury and most people have to walk a distance to obtain it. Each house has a two-acre plot of ground around it. Each person in the house uses that plot of land to plant a personal garden containing tomatoes, potatoes and maize. These houses cost about $7,500 to build, so the sisters do lots of fund raising.

Having been warned that it was dangerous to drive through the hills after dark because bandits hold up cars and buses to rob them, we left the compound intent on getting back to Lusaka before dark.

Zambia, 2009 – Sister Margie:

When I walked through one after another of the compounds in Lusaka, Zambia, the sisters with me would say, "Sister Margie will just come back with even louder sighs than before, which never seem to end." My sighs were deep breaths given out audibly that expressed a reality from deep within searing my very soul. The unimaginable reality of such extreme poverty being experienced by so many people throughout Zambia thrust me into a reality of human suffering so deep that it is difficult to wrap my mind and heart around it.

Walking through these compounds and seeing the scarcity of necessities like water, food and adequate housing is immediately evident. The dirt-floored, one room shacks made of straw are crowded together and there is one common toilet in the compound for a hundred or more people, with no water to even wash hands. Cooking is done outside. Mothers of as many as five or more children are found sitting outside their shacks attempting a smile beyond the illness and depression surrounding them.

In the midst of this most-dire situation we were met with graciousness, smiles and always greetings accompanied by a slight curtsy and small clap of hands. Children surrounded me wanting their picture taken. When they saw their picture they shouted with joy and said, "Is that me?" Since they have no mirrors nor was any other furniture to be seen, they had seen themselves for the first time.

I experienced the people's gentleness and kindness. I also perceived their deep pain in struggling to survive. The survival rate is low which leaves many orphaned children. This is compounded by tribal beliefs and actions which leave these people vulnerable, especially the women and children. In order to support themselves, vulnerable women and children may end up in prostitution or become targets of the human trafficking trade.

The conditions are such that survival is almost magical and beyond comprehension. Nothing exists that cannot be redeemed. Is a country that has over 65 percent of its population living in poverty beyond hope?

The purpose of our trip to Zambia was to focus upon one point of hope, that being the ministry of the sisters. We went to journey spiritually and psychologically with the Missionary Sisters and their lay ministry partners who are finding their lives by giving their lives away to those living on the margins of Zambian society. They are women who are sacrificing comfort, health, security, family, safety and financial security. They come from their Franciscan, Presentation, Holy Spirit and Incarnate Word community houses in Ireland, Germany, Italy, America and Zambia. They came for retreat from their ministry areas within Zambia, namely Lusaka, Mazabuka, Pemba, Solwezi and Mongu. Also, several traveled to retreat from the Congo and Zimbabwe.

The sisters attending the week-long Wholeness/Holiness Retreats came with a need to rest, relax, deepen their spirit of hope and gain renewed dedication to their difficult ministries. They wished to renew their deep love of Jesus and willingness to follow in His footsteps in reaching out to the poorest of the poor. I made the retreat right along with the sisters. They were truly models of discipleship that took away my sighs of deep pain only to be replaced with shouts of praise and thanksgiving to God for inspiring such love and service in these women of grace reaching out to the people of Zambia. Awe, wonder and hope still swell within me. These are some of the works these sisters are performing:

- Home-based care is performed by itinerant women visiting compounds and isolated villages includes tending to the needs of medicine, education, counseling, nutrition, grieving and referral. While praying with the people, they are tending to their spiritual, emotional and physical needs. Sisters often bring people to hospitals from long distances.
- They have built a village of small four-room houses with small plots of land for planting food and caring for a few animals. A second village is being built. Homeless women raising children are given first priority. The village has a common well

and is near enough to school for the children to walk.

- Operate a mobile clinic that reaches out over 200 miles, bringing medicine and food to those who are isolated without transportation or health care.
- Staff a small hospital with little or no funding, as the poor are not able to pay for service. Many sick are found sleeping on the hospital grounds waiting for room inside. Pregnant women sit on a wall outside waiting until it's time to deliver their child.
- Training for midwifery in order to deliver babies in the isolated areas.
- Establishing orphanages for children whose parents have died from the AIDS pandemic.
- Setting up a trade school for orphaned youth that offers classes in sewing, computer skills, carpentry, plumbing, metal working, cooking, gardening, and raising chickens to sell for profit.
- Teaching school with as many as sixty-two children in a small classroom. Imagine this condition in the hot season.
- Purchasing land to divide into small parcels and given to homeless families along with a small house. They are also given animals to raise and seeds to plant maize. Building a dam in order to preserve water during the rainy season.
- Directing a house of formation for novices from all religious communities.
- Planting and tending a banana plantation to finance the house of formation.
- Building an orphanage called, The Cheshire Home in Mongu, for disabled children who are unable to be cared for by their parents. They assist in building homes for these disabled

children until they turn sixteen. Then they find caretakers for many of the children whose families live isolated from any medical care. Most extended families do not have resources to care for their disabled relatives.

- Tutoring children to keep up their grades and stay in school.
- Giving workshops for lay leaders in the parish.
- Building schools in compounds, training teachers, giving classes in hygiene, providing food, medicine and transportation. Children are tutored before school, given a meal and walk several miles to school. One hundred children were placed in schools because of the intervention of one Franciscan Sister. Another sister is duplicating this work in a compound on the other side of Lusaka.
- Building a dwelling for ten orphans suffering from AIDS.

**Comments from the Sisters who attended the
Wholeness/Holiness Retreats:**

"I acknowledge that my experience in this retreat was truly Wholeness/Holiness because of the sameness of the two dimensions within myself. I'm very grateful to God and to the sponsorship I received in order to participate in a wonderful time that renewed my inner self."

"I recognize that a key for the successful results of this retreat was the direction of Sr. Margie and Sr. Connie. I'm going back to my reality and normal life with a new spirit, strength and full of hope."

"I came to Assisi House to make this retreat feeling physically sick, emotionally devastated and psychologically exhausted. Today, I leave Assisi House feeling whole! Thank you, Sisters Connie and Margie, for helping me to be whole again and for opening my eyes to a new way of BEING. I go back to my ministry, to do the same work but differently. I know how to care for myself in order to care for others more."

"I came to this retreat of Wholeness/Holiness as a bent person. I had carried a lot of burdens. I was able to off-load all that when I was being directed and in the group sharing. I want to testify to all that I am not the same person. I have let go of all that was troubling me. From the inside of me, God has worked wonders and I feel free, free and free. I am a new person. I see myself as precious, self-confident, strong and I love myself. I will always trust in my Lord. He is with me, in me and me in him."

"I came to this Wholeness/Holiness retreat feeling worn out, washed away and almost breaking. I wondered what this retreat would do for me. I tell you, Jesus had his own night time. For me, this was my night time because I had carried so much grief in my life and this was a big drawback. I lost three brothers and my Mom and Dad. I did not know how to cope. These six days of journeying with Margie and Connie brought so much healing. It was like I was broken in two pieces and each day's journey was bringing the disintegrated parts of me together. The group therapy and group direction helped me a lot to share openly. I cried and sobbed. When I went for individual direction and therapy, I was soothed. I feel gratitude within my heart for the help I got from this retreat. I am now ready within myself to walk the journey ahead. I will continue the journey. It is so soothing, healing and quieting."

"I am forty-three years old. I am a science teacher and principal at a high school for girls. These are days I will live to remember because they were grace-filled days. I came into the retreat not only riding a storm but actually in the storm. I was feeling crushed and disintegrated. My flesh and my soul were tired from the demands of my ministry and the difficult events of my life that I had not processed for years.

When I heard about the retreat on Wholeness/Holiness, I was attracted to go. I actually needed counseling and spiritual direction. When I am whole, then I could be holy. Praying and journeying with Sr. Connie and Sr. Margie this week was very life-giving in that I had my eyes opened to see what I needed to let go of and what I needed to hold on to in order to become freed and become that vibrant woman that God wants me to be. I also came to learn and realize that all the resources I need to grow and build myself up are within me. I have power to allow myself to be transformed. I also learned a lot from the wisdom of the women in the group whose sharings were very open. These women have suffered but are very strong and still love their God so much. God was also very alive for me in this retreat because I felt that God met me where I was. There has been a deep yearning in my heart to be in the now for that is where God is. The way the Wholeness and Holiness were integrated helped me to be counseled and to pray. I come out of this retreat feeling much energized, empowered to walk again with new eyes and new wisdom. The transformation process has startled me. I desire it and it is happening and it has happened."

"I thank Sisters Margie and Connie for their wisdom on whose shoulders I have stood. I thank Krista, Christine, Evan, Loontia, Zennobia and Josephine whose openness in sharing their stories enriched me and made me wiser. I thank the Presentation Sisters for their generosity in organizing this retreat and finding sponsorship. To all of you, I say, 'You lifted me higher than I could ever fly.'"

"This retreat has been an extraordinary experience for me, and once more, I have touched God's love in an unexpected way. Like a lover He comes with surprises. I would like to use the symbol of a kite to express this powerful moment in my life.

"Before retreat I felt like a kite trying to fly high but my tail and frame were dragging me toward the earth. I was nose-diving into the ground as life's strong winds and challenges tossed me around. After a week of being in the Spirit's strong winds of grace, I feel I am being carried into the blue skies of love and healing with my tail waving and my frame rejuvenated. I am ready to dance like a feather being tossed about in a gentle breeze. God is holding on to the string of my life. I am free to fly wherever the Spirit leads me."

"And the "holy ones" go forth transforming their limitations into enlargements and all adversity into opportunities of amazing grace."

*SISTER MARGIE HOSCH, OSF, SISTER CONNIE FAHEY, FSM,
MARY CATHERINE HARRIS, BILL HANCOCK*

Sister Connie at home after her first trip to Zambia:

The thirty days I spent in the presence of women from India, Ireland, Zambia, the Congo, Zimbabwe, Micronesia, Mexico and Italy was definitely a unique retreat experience. One doesn't have to go into seclusion to experience the awesome power and compassion of God! During those days I experienced sisters' cavernous depths of love as I walked through the dusty, dirty roads of compounds with sisters who have given their one, precious life to serve Zambia's marginalized peoples. I witnessed to women's pain as they mourned deaths of multiple family members. As each woman shared her sea of pain with me, I was aware that she was touching the shores of my compassion; we were on holy ground as the Spirit of God touched and healed her soul. As I experienced the unrelenting and all-encompassing poverty around me, I wondered about how the magnanimity of a few valiant women was able to bring hope and joy to the hungry, destitute people, victimized by sickness and few resources. As I return home to the cleanliness of my apartment with hot water, electricity and plenty of food and the assurances of safety in my neighborhood, my prayer is:

> Open my senses to wisdom's inner promptings
> that I may give voice to what I hear in my soul
> and be changed for the healing of the world,
> that I may listen for truth in every living soul
> and be changed for the well-being of the world.
> Taken from: *Sounds of the Eternal; A Celtic Psalter;*
> *Author J. Philop Newell*

Sister Margie at home after her first trip to Zambia:

Upon arriving home from Zambia, I was met by a gathering of donor friends at the airport to welcome me home. They invited me to my own apartment where they had set up snacks and drinks. They sat for two hours to assist me in debriefing the daring and crazy journey that edged me closer to God, who embraces all the living by using us to do the embracing. Community truly happens as we unfold our lives to one another.

Because of the generosity of friends and other donors a contribution was made to the Presentation Sisters for the purpose of helping to build a small house for Anna Selembe. She was left at the doorstep of the Presentation orphanage called "Cheshire Home" in Mongu. Anna was severely handicapped and couldn't be cared for by her impoverished family. During her eight years there, Anna was given extensive physiotherapy in an effort to make her mobile, which unfortunately wasn't possible.

Anna's relatives are living in an extremely remote and poor area north of Lukulu with absolutely no means or way of caring for a severely handicapped woman on a 24-hour basis. They walk very long distances to find water for their needs and hygiene becomes a major problem especially in the very hot weather. Food is in short supply and the woman doing the constant caring leaves Anna alone for long periods of time to access food and water.

Anna is one of hundreds of young people in this situation. In an effort to support some of their past children from Cheshire Home, including Anna, who are severely disabled, the sisters are trying to set them up with low cost two-room houses with some facilities such as running water nearby to make full-time care more possible and somewhat easier. They hire caretakers to live with the young handicapped people on a 24-hour basis.

Provision of clean drinking water is one of the Millennium Development Goals for Zambia. This is yet very far from becoming a reality in Western Zambia where the Council system is unable to supply even the needs of the immediate Township. Any outlying areas have absolutely no supply or may have water for one hour per week. The sisters have people to set up water systems which then can be piped to the small houses for the disabled. Let the dreamers come. If we dream it we may be able to accomplish it. We trust that this future will unfold. But for now, just know the bricks that are building Anna's home are paid for.

On their first trip Sisters Margie and Connie conducted 3 Retreats for 18 Sisters.

Chapter Four
Why Be a Pilgrim Still?
...There is more to see and much more to do

Zambia, 2010 – Sister Connie:

Returning to Africa the second time was far less stressful than my first trip. Sister Margie and I knew where we were going and we knew the sisters we would be staying with during this month-long visit, the Franciscan Missionary Sisters of Assisi. But even though our anticipations for this trip were less stressful, we were unsure about how we would be received by the over one hundred sisters who were registered to attend the seminars we had prepared for them. We were instructed to prepare three seminars for junior professed Zambian Sisters and one traditional Wholeness/Holiness Retreat during the last week of our stay for eight Zambian Sisters.

Our seminar was based on the resiliencies of five women in Scripture. Each day, Sister Margie presented the component elements of resilience which are needed to live a vibrant and healthy life and I presented a Scripture woman who exhibited the resiliency. So the seminar was part instruction, part reflection, part time for discussion and plenty of time for rest and relaxation for the participants. The seminar was held in Kalundu, a central site for formation of Zambian Sisters. It was attended by one hundred and twenty sisters from twenty-two congregations who ministered in most of Zambia's provinces. The seminars were exhilarating both for the participants and us two facilitators as well.

It was a great joy and inspiration to be among those young women who are beginning their life as women religious in a country which is fraught with overwhelming challenges. They live in dire poverty, work among the poorest of poor and straddle a world between their own upbringing in tribal life and religious life as we knew it in the1950's and 1960's.

They are the ones who are building an infrastructure of hospitals and schools to serve their own people. I was reminded of my own youthful enthusiasm and idealism as I spent time listening to their stories of courage and selfless services for children, elderly, victims of violence, tribal customs and the devastating disease of AIDS.

We walked with them through an orphanage which housed, fed and educated two hundred and fifty children. While there, we listened to their stories of how they were mothering these beautiful children through their growing up years.

We saw their dedication as they nursed sick and dying patients in a Hospice which is staffed by persons who were being treated for the AIDS virus, heard how they did continuous world-wide fundraising to keep the institution running and listened to their fears of being cut-off from United States funding for the medicines. These medicines are needed to treat the disease for three thousand clients they are serving in one of the ten disease catchment areas of Luaska.

These women serve out in the bush country where electricity, running water, and the comforts of modern society have not permeated the environs of their lives. They are pragmatic, fun-loving, great singers and dancers. All are trying to figure out how to live life to the fullest in the midst of scratching around for their daily living needs.

Sister Connie at home after the second trip to Zambia:

I went to Zambia the second time to share a bit of my knowledge of spirituality with Zambian women of religious life. I returned home refreshed in my own call to religious life knowing that there are many young women on the other side of the world who are "joyful in hope, patient in affliction and faithful in prayer," (Romans 12:12) because I witnessed their amazing zest and compassion for God's beloved children living in dire poverty.

While I was in Zambia, I missed the comforts of accessible clean water, dependable hot showers, navigable paved roads and bug-free housing. However, I came home with a deep knowing that God's church and people are found not only in beautiful buildings like St. John Vianney's parish (my Janesville parish's name) but also in compounds, hospices and orphanages housing the vulnerably sick and poor of Zambia.

On one of my first days home I went to Mass at my parish. It was a sunny, spring Thursday morning, a day when the children of the parish's school attend Mass. I was sitting in the back of church observing the astounding beauty of the children as they filed into the pews dressed in their school colors of red and khaki. They were so self-assured, so clean, so amazingly competent as they announced and read the day's readings and sang hymns befitting the liturgy.

The sight of St. John Vianney's children overwhelmed me and I suddenly found myself transported back to the Kasisi parish in Zambia where I also sat in the back of the parish church and witnessed a hundred or more orphans filing into another church and taking their seats on the wooden benches in front of me. They were dressed nicely; their brown faces shiny clean and their African hair neatly braided or tied in bows. The tiny ones sat on the front benches and hardly wiggled during the long Mass while the older boys and girls sat behind them doing what teenagers usually do, acting bored.

During the previous week, I had toured the orphanage located adjacent to the retreat Center where we were conducting a retreat for Zambian women religious. The orphanage had a dozen buildings housing various age groups of children, newborn through teenagers. The tiny babies were in bassinets and cribs, the older children slept in rows of beds in dormitories. As we walked through the various dormitory living spaces, we noted that each bed was neatly made with a furry animal on each pillow. Two or three women lived with the children in their dorms and were on duty caring for their fifty or so children day and night. The orphanage has a small hospice to care for a few children who have succumbed to the ravages of the AIDS disease. The women religious managing the orphanage have given their life to protect these children who are the victims of Zambia's huge AIDS epidemic.

The magnitude of the implications of the Zambian experience of one orphanage came crashing in on me as I observed the St. John Vianney's children, as I observed delightfully healthy, vibrant children filing into pews in front of me. What if it were these St. John Vianney's children sitting in front of me who were the orphans? Would we allow those children to live in an institution with surrogate mothers to nurture them, care for them in their illnesses, and love them into adulthood? Why does God allow this kind of pain and suffering in our world? And what if many of the children that were in front of me had the AIDS virus in their beautiful bodies? What kind of care can one woman give to the more frail ones among the fifty or more children she cares for on a 24/7 basis? What responsibility do I have even though I am neither a Zambian nor even a parent?

When one is sitting in a clean home, with running water and dependable electricity, it is easy to ignore the claim the poor have upon one or rationalize that it is someone else's problem. Therefore, it is a problem that I have no responsibility to solve or to be involved in. But even as I rationalize myself out of the situation, I saw two hundered fifty blessed and privileged children sitting in front of me and was challenged to at least tell the story, to describe the situation in such a way that a few hearts may be stirred with compassion. Oscar Romero said, "We cannot do everything and there is a sense of liberation in realizing this because this enables us to do something." *Opous Die* (Work of God)

I wonder what the "something" may be for me. I may not be able to give each child a home and loving parents, but maybe, just maybe, I can stir others' hearts to pray for the children, especially the immense number of parentless children sentenced to a life of deprivation because of their parent's ignorance about a devastating disease. I will continue to not only keep them in mind and heart, but will tell their story so someone will plead the cause of the least among us. And if I return to Zambia next year, I hope to take some financial aid for the sisters who have given their lives in this daunting ministry. There are many Mother Teresas running around Zambia.

Without getting too technical, I've come to a painful realization that all is not well when we have such huge disparities between children living in Janesville, Wisconsin and those living in Kasisi, Zambia.

> *Who will succor the homeless, the orphans, the starving,*
> *those cast aside by decisions based on greed?*
> *Who will speak up on their behalf?*
> *Let all with faith-filled hearts rise*
> *up with Love!*
> Psalm 83

Sister Margie at home after the second trip to Zambia:

Taking flight is a common adventure when we have the means and modern methods to keep us airborne. An airplane is made to fly. Passengers are content to trust their safety within its structured design. All the machinations needed to keep the plane in the air are patterned and designed to fly us to our destinations.

We are spiritually patterned to fly in our desire to reach the lands of our sisters and brothers in the impoverished places of Zambia. We have received all the spiritual machinations needed to be present to our sisters and brothers living in the most dire of circumstances and to receive the grace of their sacrificial love for their people.

It is God's gift of presence within them that enables them to minister to those with so much pain and suffering, starvation and sickness, abuse and deprivation of all kinds. Now we know how these missionary sisters and brothers in Zambia maintain their refusal to fly away. Their fuel tanks of grace will not fly them away but are decelerating enough for them to land. Their fuel is the fire in their souls to remain grounded to their people.

I have been pondering how we are designed to fly, since returning from two missions to Zambia. How can these missionary sisters and the people they serve maintain any faith in flying when they remain grounded with so much pain, suffering, starvation, sickness, abuse and deprivation of all kinds? Where is their airspeed of faith?

I found it when I stood with these sisters, hearing their stories and being a witness to their comforting presence to those dying of AIDS, carrying the orphans over the thresholds of their orphanage after finding them abandoned there, driving for hundreds of miles in their four-wheel drive vehicles to deliver babies, to provide new mothers with medical supplies, to build small houses for the abused women and their children, providing a common well for the impoverished population with proceeds from benefactors, hearing the drumbeat of their prayers and dancing of their spirits that never seem to die.

Believe me, the sisters are flying. We had thirty-nine sisters on each of the three seminars and eight sisters on the retreat. The sisters were representative of fourteen religious communities, eight international and six Zambian communities. They came to the seminars and retreat that we gave with a deep desire to find a renewal of spirit that keeps them believing in themselves and the empowerment of the Spirit within.

A few sisters came at the beginning of the retreat with their suitcases packed and ready to leave their communities, some with deep depression, burnout and lack of hope. Some came experiencing authoritarian leadership adopted from tribal cultures which transferred and applied to religious life. Each of the sisters had malaria with multiple recurrences. Most were ridden with a form of poverty of our time, no one to love them in their own uniqueness while giving their lives away for others.

Throughout each week we journeyed with the women in Scripture, with the resiliencies they manifested in their relationship with Jesus and ways each sister could live out these resiliencies in addressing the social issues of the religions, in their ministries and within their religious communities. But, most of all, the sisters made application to their own self care.

We sang, beat the drums, shook the shakers, danced, celebrated liturgies in Zambian style, created personal manifestos of changes we wished to make, reconciled our past hurts and failures, then cleared our spirits of damaging thinking that kept us from receiving the love of Jesus and one another. Each sister stood and proclaimed the person she had become in a creative expression of herself before leaving the support of the group.

Wow! Suitcases were repacked with empowerment, forgiveness, strength, love and with the "airspeed of faith" to carry on. Everyone returned with a recommitment to continue to follow Jesus to the compounds, into the hospitals, to homes of the sick, into the streets of dirt where children play. They continue to construct street schools for children too poor to go to school, to care for orphans and to bring medication to those living in the bush. They promised to be a listening presence to each sister in their times of need.

These Zambian sisters went forward, believing they had the power to fly. We go forward believing we have the power to fly by being carried by the power of the Spirit within us to those with whom we live, by feeding the hungry, housing the homeless, comforting those who are sorrowing, praying with the sick, listening to the heartbeat of another's pain and providing hope just because we are ready to listen and care deeply for each person whose story we take time to hear.

I end with an e-mail from a missionary sister in Zambia whose story was told and held sacred. She writes, "Thank you for journeying with me during the confusion of my life. I am now back in school and taking whatever is coming my way as it comes. Sister, be ever my companion in my prayer life. I am remembering you in my feeble prayers."

On their second trip Sisters Margie and Connie conducted Seminars for 106 Sisters and a Retreat for 8 Sisters.

Mary Catherine Harris: Coming to meet Sister Margie Hosch.

To Sister Margie Hosch and the Wholeness/Holiness Retreat in South Carolina during 2010, I brought my wounded, broken self in the aftermath of a divorce that had ended my marriage of close to forty-two years. Crushed emotionally and spiritually, I also carried in my chest the unrelenting physical sensation of a cold hardness.

A lifetime of knowing about God and participating in the Church, along with years of education and experience as a teacher and counselor, had proven insufficient to meet my deep need in this heavy and burdensome time. I wanted to live and live fully and I believed it to be possible; I knew I needed help.

During a late-night, somewhat desperate internet search for resources for women in divorce recovery, information about the Wholeness/Holiness Retreat entered my radar and seemed to spell my name. It was described as integrating spiritual and psychological aspects for women in transition or crisis or ordinary life, for developing a new sense of inner strength, self-nurturing and empowerment to make necessary changes to bring healing and growth for living more fulfilling lives. Who couldn't benefit from that? For me, it seemed more than a matter of benefit. I needed what it offered.

In this time of my life when trust did not come easily, there came from somewhere the feeling that I could trust what lay ahead in this experience. (Trasna moment!) From the first moments of the Retreat, it was clear to me that I could trust this gifted spirit-filled leader. As I began to feel heard, affirmed and embraced by both Margie and the other women in the retreat group, I felt also a disintegration of the sense of abandonment and inferiority that had begun to settle in since my divorce. It was as if I were being transported from the alien territory where I had been cast and taken into a home space that was better than I last remembered of home. I felt loved by and connected with God in a new and unique way, and I began to feel empowered for the journey ahead. I began to love God's beloved creation that was and is Mary Catherine.

Openness to new life, I began to realize, meant openness to my deepest truth. Gently yet firmly, Margie led me to recognize and acknowledge feelings and beliefs and behaviors and my denial of them, that were hindering my life and had, in fact, hindered my life prior to divorce. Each step toward who I truly am, sometimes unlike who I appear to be or think I am, was then and continues to be a step into refreshing freedom.

When I started home at the end of the retreat, my spirit seemed as light as a feather and the heaviness in my chest had noticeably disappeared. It was snowing at the time and I knew travel could be risky. I remember thinking that even if I did not reach home safely, I could rest in gratitude that in those days I had come to peace in a way unlike any I had ever known. It was as if I had come home to myself in God.

Sharing such a profound experience is difficult and risky but, yes, I did share. On one hand, it is almost too deep and sacred to touch. On the other hand, it is almost beyond what another can take in. My daughters were grateful to learn that from the retreat I was experiencing some healing from the heartbreak of divorce. I think I may have been somewhat guarded in what I exposed to them, wanting to protect them from worry about me and also from any aspect of the retreat experience that could impact negatively their relationship with their dad.

All my friends were relieved to know the retreat had been helpful. I remember sharing more in depth and detail with a couple of friends. One was an older woman in my church who had expressed unusual care for me and who invited me to visit and share the retreat experience with her and her caregiver. She was able to take what I described and apply it to some degree to a heartbreaking circumstance from her own life. She expressed happiness that life seemed brighter for me.

Another friend, whom I knew to be seriously engaged in spiritual seeking, invited me to share the retreat experience with her. Trusting her capability to receive and also her protection of privacy, I was able to express in a similar manner with her. She seemed a bit in awe, but also somewhat understanding of the process. She, too, seemed grateful.

Again, the sharing is a paradox of wanting to shout it to the world while also sensing that you don't dare. Holding that tension, I shared then and continue to share now, however and with whomever feels right in the moment.

My experience in the Wholeness/Holiness Retreat was the beginning of healing. Additionally, it set me on a course of deep spiritual seeking that continues to comfort, amaze and excite me. I returned to the retreat twice more as a participant and from there began hosting retreats for women in my home, with Margie leading. My desire was then and is now to be an agent in providing this life-giving experience to others.

My hunger and thirst for all things spiritual led me into a course of training which ended in certification in spiritual direction. This has provided tremendous enrichment for my personal journey, while also equipping and preparing me to be a more attentive spiritual companion for others.

Chapter Five
The Voice Continues Calling
...Many children are running the streets

Zambia, 2011 – Sister Connie:

We arrived in Lusaka on Thursday, June 30th and went to work immediately. We gave the thirty sisters from twenty-three congregations and ten African countries studying at the Kalundu Study Center a day of reflection. We met with a couple of Theresian Sisters who want us to come to Malawi next year and give their sisters retreats.

Over the weekend we went to the Poor Clare Monastery for liturgy. We were joined by Dr. Ben Asen from St. Louis University; he was there to give the Kalundu Sisters a week-long intensive study on The Prophets. We had a nice time talking about mutual friends at SLU. The liturgy at the Poor Clares was just the beginning of a series of liturgical experiences of Divine Presence among the people of God. We will be going back to the Poor Clare Monastery next year to give thirty-seven sisters Wholeness/Holiness Retreats.

On July 5th we were driven to Solwezi by Bishop Charles Kasonde's right hand man, Father Neal Mulyata. We broke the ten hour trip up by stopping along the way at Wimpy's, a McDonald-like place for ice cream. Margie loves ice cream! Upon getting to the Solwezi Diocese we stopped to see Father Vincent and hear his story. He is the shepherd of people living a couple hundred miles in the bush country. His parish center is at St. Dorothy with twenty-one outposts or small Christian communities in the bush country. Sunday collection amounts to $2.00 and a few chickens; we left him some money and pencils. He was beyond grateful; it meant he would eat better for the next few weeks and the kids would have something to write with as they did their lessons in unbelievably primitive buildings without books to help them learn to read, write or do arithmatic.

Then we proceeded to the Solwezi Diocesan Center where we were housed for the rest of the month. The diocese has a guest house and we were welcomed by the staff on a daily basis as they took care of our physical needs for the month. It wasn't the Marriott, but it was clean and we had hot water and electricity most of the time and adequate sustenance for our bodies.

The week before the retreats we toured a couple of sites in the bush country and the Diocesan Project offices. They included Youth Ministry, HIV/AIDS and Home Bound Health Services office, Business Development office, Legal office, Diocesan Management offices and a pre-school for street children which shares space with the public school.

Sister Norma, a Mercedarian Sister, teaches children on park benches in the yard and uses the church building wall to hang her lessons on for the children to learn about rudimentary topics. A child cannot go to the public school if they don't have shoes, a uniform, tuition and school supplies. It costs $200/child/year, so the diocese is able to support seventeen children through twelve years of schooling if they stay in school. Thousands of children run the streets of Solwezi because they don't have parents or their parents don't have resources or they may be housed and fed by relatives but the relatives have no money to educate them. We visited several homes of children the diocese is helping to get a rudimentary education. The homes had electric power from car batteries; they can't afford electricity from the city.

We went to one of the six Diocesan Health Centers in Chisassa, an hour and half drive from Solwezi. There we saw how sister nurses run a Health Clinic with little or no medicines or supplies, no physician guidance and limited electricity and water supplies. Unbelievable! They do about twenty deliveries a month and first aid for people who come in. They have an ambulance that they use to transport patients to a small hospital in Solwezi. I doubt if there is any place in the US that is working with the kind of scarce resources these women work with in Chisassa. The hospital has a generator but they don't use it much because they can't afford the petrol to run it. So, when it gets dark they use candles.

We began a retreat on July 12th for eighteen sisters from six congregations. It was a delight to get to know them. Most of them were very young but there were a few older sisters attending who were most appreciative of the days of reflection and camaraderie. The retreats were held at the St. Kizitos Pastoral Center in Solwezi, a newly developed Center of Diocesan pastoral and catechetical education.

Over the weekend, Bishop Kasonde took us to two Confirmation liturgies. On Saturday, we went to Kafumbwe about 10 miles from town and Sunday to St. Kitzitos in town. When Bishop Kasonde arrived at the church in Kafumbwe the children and women did an elaborate dance laying their chitangas (wrap-around like aprons) on

the ground for Bishop Kasonde to walk on as he proceeded to the church, a simple brick walled building with a tin roof and openings on all sides to the nature around it. Since there is no vestry in which Bishop Kasonde could put on his vestments, he vested from the trunk of his 4-wheel drive truck.

The Africans know how to celebrate liturgy; each one lasted 4-5 hours and there was much dancing and wonderful singing. The Gloria lasted about half-an-hour as they sang and danced it. The Bishop later told us he was watching us in the back of the church sitting among the women and children as the offertory procession progressed. The procession is another extended period event. It was led by the Stellas (a group of little girls 5-10 years old) doing intricate dance steps while the congregation sang melodious songs in 4 or 5 part harmonies in their native tongue and drummers beat out soul-stirring rhythms on drums of various sizes and tones.

The offering procession consists of people bringing up their gifts consisting of goats, chickens, roosters, various food products and large bags of milli-meal. The Bishop distributed the ten goats, numerous chickens and other food gifts received among his parishes for their food supply.

After the Confirmation in Kafubwe, we had dinner with Bishop Kasonde and parish leader at the village chief's house. The meal consisted of roast chicken, a green spinach-like vegetable and nshema, a staple food that is like solid cream-of-wheat. So we ate like natives using our fingers, no utensils, and using the nshema to hold the liquidy vegetables together.

The following week, Monday July 18th, we started the priests retreat. This was an application of the Wholeness/Holiness Retreat program to men for the first time. Margie and I had more than a little trepidation before we started the retreat because we did not know what to expect. But wow! What a wonderful group of men!

There were twenty-seven in the group, the oldest was 53 years old and the five deacons who were to be ordained the next week were the youngest.

It doesn't take much to inspire another or for that matter, to scandalize another person. Small actions are like small pebbles thrown in a pond; the ripple effects are not foreseen nor can they be predicted. An incident happened after the completion of the retreat for the Solwezi women religious.

Sister Margie used her photographic skills to portray nature's beauty and gently invite retreatants into the realm of their spirit by reflecting upon the nature's beauty and how the picture speaks to her soul. Pictures are literally worth a thousand words because the connection between a person and the observed beauty of the photograph has a ripple effect not only on the person who is responding to the beauty portrayed in the photo but also because when a woman shares her unique beauty with the group everyone sees God's beauty in a new way. And as a person shares a snippet of their story all in the group are able to see the reverberation of God's beauty in our small earthly selves.

Upon the completion of the women's retreat, we left the photographs on the table in the front room without much thought about how these same pictures might appeal to the next group of retreatants; the Solwezi diocese priests. As stated, Sister Margie and I were apprehensive because we had not given the retreat to men before, let alone to priests.

As the priests arrived for their time of reflection, the first thing they noticed was the pictures that we had left on the table. As one by one they came into the room, they were immediately attracted to the pictures lying on the table. The Spirit was at work. We saw that not only had the women seen the beauty in the photographs but also the men's spirits were being touched. So whatever anxiety we had about moving into a new experience of giving a retreat with these special men was greatly allayed.

We had rediscovered that humans have much in common and beauty calls upon beauty. As John O'Donohue says in his book *Beauty: The Invisable Embrace,* "We were sent into the world alive with beauty. As soon as we choose beauty, unseen forces conspire to guide and encourage us towards unexpected forms of compassion, healing and creativity."

The priests' evaluations of our retreat time with them speak volumes about the beauty of each man that we had the privilege to serve as facilitators of their special time together. Here are some of the evaluation quotes from the priests who took the retreat.

- The presentation was good and I request that they may come again next year.

- The programme of on-going formation was very enriching, most especially that it helped me to revive my drooping spirit.

- Personally, it was a great moment of brotherly sharing and self-discovery. As far as I know, this was the first ever for all religious and clergy to meet and pray together. I urge that this ought to be done as often as means may allow. I bemoan the absence of those who did not make it to this great time.

- The retreat was ok, though the time was not enough. We could have done or learned more. The facilitation was good. God bless the sisters!

- I had time to re-visit my vocation. I found that the talks and exercises preached to me. I have been preaching to others for a long time without being preached to.

- The days have been full of meaning and inspiration. Our spirits were rocked!

The two retreats were as enriching, inspiring and renewing for us as for those who participated in them.We took fifty books with us to hand out to the retreatants. The books were like gold for the sisters and priests. They have very little access to good reading materials, so we had Christmas in July as we gave them the books along with the pencils and rosaries.

Following the retreats, we visited with the various groups of sisters in Solwezi, enjoying a meal, hearing their stories and renewing friendships from our former visits. We went to St. Steven's parish, a new church managed by Father Chris and Sister Lucy, on Sunday and were welcomed by the people of the parish. We must have shaken hands with two hundred men, women and children as they curtsied and welcomed us into their new worship space. Returning, we traveled on a few paved roads that had potholes as big as bathtubs and on rutted, dusty roads at 5 miles-per-hour and arrived back in Solwezi with dust in our hair, on our clothes and grit in our teeth.

We visited several schools including a premier school run by the Baptistine Sisters. They have few books and scarce resources to use for the learning experience of the children. One day we stopped to watch prisioners take down a huge ant hill behind the guest house, using a pick ax and hoes. The clay left behind by the ants will be used to make bricks.

We had a delightful time visiting with Bishop Charles Kasonde, who didn't take a day off all the time we were there. He told us about his people throughout the diocese and the many challenges facing him as he encourages, cajoles, begs and humors his priests, sisters and laity to take hold of the church of Solwezi and make it their church. He loves his people and they love him.

The Catholic Diocese of Solwezi was established in 1976. It is a vast diocese and one of the biggest in Africa. The Catholic population of ninety-thousand is thinly scattered over a land area of 78,185 square miles. There are three dominant languages in that area, with English spoken mainly by the educated population. The newly initiated Roman Missal has to be translated into three languages to serve the people of this diocese, not to say anything about the other dioceses in Zambia.

Due to political disturbances in the Democratic Republic of Congo, Rwanda and Angola there is a large influx of refugees that the diocese serves. There is a camp with a large refugee population located about an hour's ride outside of Solwezi. The diocese is predominantly rural and very poor; more than sixty percent live in extreme poverty. One of the priests told us that sometimes a family of six has three people eat one meal on one day and the other three eat a meal the next day. Can you imagine being this poor?

The roads in the diocese are rough, mostly un-tarred making access to most of the outlying church communities difficult and almost impossible during the rainy season during November through April. Bishop Kasonde and his priests drive four-wheel drive trucks to navigate the dirt and sand roads in the bush country. There are thirty-four clerics and seventy religious men and women who

run 20 parishes along with 394 smaller church mission sites, 6 mission hospitals, 2 leprosaria, 3 homes for physically and mentally challenged persons, 18 kindergarten schools, 4 grade schools and 3 craft (technical) centers.

While we were at the Solwezi Diocesan Center, Sister Krista, the Bishop's secretary, kept us in cookies and soda, but we didn't have a bottle opener so we substituted water at our little break parties until we were able to borrow a bottle opener from Bishop Kasonde's kitchen. The night before we left to come home we had dinner with Bishop Kasonde and told him that we would try to get a few dollars to help meet the needs of the priests and sisters of the diocese. They receive no salary or stipend for their labors and must depend on the poor they serve to feed them and know Bishop Kasonde will help them when they are in dire need.

On July 27th Father Neal drove us along with four seminarians from Solwezi to Ndola. The seminarians were going to have their ordination cards printed at the Franciscan Printing press in Ndola in preparation for ordination coming up on August 13th. They were very excited about the coming event. We asked them how long the liturgy lasted for an ordination. They replied that it lasts at least six hours and the number of goats and chickens received will be a great number.

In Ndola, we stopped to have tea/coffee at the Franciscan Sisters of Assisi Province House before going to the airport. When I walked into the house, the Provincial was simply astounded that I came; she had been trying to find my address to thank me for what St. Mary's Hospital in Madison, WI did for one of their sisters. That was one of those serendipitous happenings that is almost spooky. After a nice visit, we went to the airport and began our journey home.

Our route took us to Johannesburg and while there we visited with a sister who gave us a quick tour of Soweto as we were waiting to transfer to our next flight. That was quite another experience; to see where history was made in South Africa.

Zambia, 2011 – Sister Margie:

"Have a banana. Have two bananas!" These words of Bishop Charles Kasonde, Bishop of the Solwezi Diocese in Zambia, were spoken from the heart, so big that he would welcome us by extending to us the only food available in his humble four-room dwelling. The whole month of July 2011, opened me to a new meaning of how we can be presented to the Divine Presence beyond any words or actions, position or power, rich or poor, broken or healed, learned or unlearned, having all the answers to questions and having no answers at all. To do this I took in the spirit of people shining through their faces and captured it on my digital camera. "For truly, the face is like an icon which expresses the spirit of the soul within." (Soulful Spirituality, David G. Brenner)

Presence has a depth that lives beneath the surface and ripples outward in the smallest and most unexpected ways. The ripples of welcome, respect, graciousness, along with a deep yearning to spend time in prayer and celebration, ushered me into a space of experiencing a people bent over by unimaginable poverty, disease and isolation, but with an energy that is vibrant with the drum beat of spirit that never seems to tire.

Their beauty of soul is transfigured in an African liturgy where

the whole body becomes an expression of freely praising God with the created gifts of voice, dance and movement, while hands and feet beat out the rhythm of heart and soul which is all guided by the drums and beautiful harmonies of their songs.

Bishop Charles Kasonde invited us to accompany him into several outposts where he presided over liturgy and confirmation. The wedding Feast of Cana had nothing over these gatherings of people who walked miles to reach their tiny churches. Water wasn't changed into wine but people's drooping spirits were lifted in praise to their Divine Chief, the God of all people, who promised them never ending life and love forever and ever.

Having few financial resources to give at the offertory, they all processed in dance down the dirt floor to the altar giving of their means which included such food items as maize, goats, chickens, vegetables, bananas and papayas. It is not surprising that these liturgies lasted over four hours because this experience is longed for by a people who can only be visited every three or four years and who sacrifice the long walk to get there and back. They give their all.

There is no 'processed welcome' by gentle shaking of the hand. The gift of two bananas became a symbol for me of the graciousness of a people pouring out a welcome beyond my imagination; I will give you what I have. In each place the whole parish danced in procession to greet and welcome us to their community. Children, youth, and adults came with tears in their eyes and their hearts in their hugs, thanking us for coming to be with them. Their holiness of spontaneity sacramented for me the embrace of our God who made us all one body, one family of Christ. Loving one another lives in the embrace of all nations, all races and creeds, working and living together as one. For truly, nothing can separate us from the love of God.

Father Richard Rohr points out in his writings that Jesus always invited the rich and powerful to 'come down' and the poor to 'come up'. What a privilege it would be to belong to each diocese, each parish, each educational institution, each organization, each family, each business, where each follower of Jesus heard the Gospel call to minister to the oppressed of the world and to say to Jesus, "Here I am, send me, I have what you need. What I have I give you. I have financial means and the talent to help YOU form the Body of Christ where no individual or nation is unduly hungry, without resources, without housing, without medicines, oppressed, and who have no place to call home."

Then places like the Diocese of Solwezi, Zambia would not be a depiction of the image I have for its extreme material poverty, namely, "Holes of the Heart." A hole is treacherous reality when found in all but one of the unguarded roads throughout the diocese. This makes access to the diocese as a whole difficult and the outstations very prohibitive. The roads leading to these places become impassable during the rainy season which lasts for about four months.

Holes exist when ten percent of the children who are fortunate to attend school often have to walk miles on dirty, muddy roads with the wind swirling the fine dust of sand in and out of those holes. The one uniform per child has to be worn for a year. During the rainy season they come to school wet, muddy and exhausted. Their little shoes never make it to the end of the school year. Hopefully parishes, families and individuals will sponsor a child in the years ahead so they can continue on to graduation.

Holes depict the empty bowls on the table where half the family eats their one and only meal and the other half of the family eats the next day. One full meal in two days after walking miles, no lunch in school and then walking back home is almost too much to take in. Two little girls came running over to us when we were visiting their outside class room saying, "Sister, we are so hungry." We witnessed the sisters taking care of the children left at school until a late hour. After being fed, the parents came to pick up their children. One can only conclude that this was a way the parents could manage to have their children receive something to eat.

We saw holes of isolation where priests are missioned singularly in order to minister to the little churches and each priest having up to sixty-five outstations. There are only trails for roads which are not passable during the rainy season. Often the isolation is exascerbated when food and water are rationed and electricity is nonexistent. Dampness brings on illness. No doctor is available if someone is sick. Clinics are not present in most places throughout the diocese.

Holes exist when we witness the hunger for spiritual reading books. There is no book store in the whole diocese. We were able to bring a spiritual book for each priest and sister on retreat and understand that there are plans at work to expand this mission and find a way to send more children to school. Sources in the states have committed to supplying some books and others are providing funding to send some children to school in Solwezi Diocese.

Upon visiting the women and children living in extreme poverty we met a little girl whose sister died of malaria. The day before returning to America we grieved with those who knew a family whose nine-month-old baby had just died of starvation. Our hearts were aching when we discovered there are no resources or established infrastructure to keep people from dying. The lifespan for an average person is thirty-five years. What do these facts ask of us? What do we do with our plenty? What do we do with the hillside full of orphans who have nothing to eat? It is up to us to multiply the loaves and fishes. Our foundress, Mother Xavier Termehr, knew what to do in Herford, Germany during the war in 1864. She gathered the orphans off the streets, gave them a home, washed, clothed and fed them and loved them into life.

The living saints of Solwezi, the bishop, priests, sisters and serving laity, respond daily with brave and courageous words when they say, "Here I am, Jesus. What I have I give to you this day." The holes within their hearts are diminished as they expand all heart space with the Infinite. Their ministry is providing an echo of God's love for all creation that is in their view. And hopefully, we are blessed to be sent from the United States and can be transfigured into a whole new way of being in the world. I see the sisters as a bridge between those who have and those who have not. In the Spirit of making nothing permanent here, we can go lightly and be a voice for the voiceless. "What you do to the least of my brothers and sisters, you do to me."

Hildegard von Bingen (1098-1179, also known as Saint Hildegard and Sibyl of the Rhine, a German Benedictine abbess, writer, composer, Christian mystic, visionary and polymath) described herself as being a feather on the breath of God. To make the most of our God-given gifts, we realize that to store them brings them to ruin, to use them and share them is to give them permanence here which lives on beyond us. We really never get God, God just gets us. And then we just get God in those given to us to love and serve. My life of love could be contained in the tiniest of thimbles compared to the lakes of love filling up the never-ending holes of those who are falling by the wayside and are in need of a good Samaritan to stop and offer help. ("They will know you are following me by your love.")

The Solwezi diocese covers the entire political-geographical Northwestern province of Zambia. There are fewer than fifty priests and sisters serving eighty-thousand Catholics thinly scattered over an extensive underdeveloped area in this province. What makes service very difficult is the existence of three tribes, with each having their own language and other minor tribes with additional languages. Isolation is devastating on the clergy who are missioned singulary and are often not in communication with others over an extended period of time. Sisters live in community, which helps them manage the isolation better.

Since over 90% of the parishes cannot contribute financially to the diocese or to the local church, Bishop Kasonde is responsible for the financial needs of the priests, some of the local communities of sisters and the development of church buildings. Sisters belonging to international communites all work without salary and are dependent upon their communities for their housing and daily living expenses. With only forty-five thousand dollars being sent to the Solwezi diocese from international collections for the global needs of the church, Bishop Kasonde must find resources in first world countries. With a sigh in his heart, he shared how difficult it is to financially support those who are studying for the priesthood.

We attended liturgy in one parish administered by Sister Lucy. When it came time to distribute the Eucharist, Father Chris gave the ciborium to sister to distribute to her people. I was spiritually lifted when I witnessed the many signs of priests and sisters working in harmony and deep respect for one another in service of the people. In one of the missions an elderly woman asked Bishop Kasonde for permission to speak to the people. Bishop Kasonde listened and gave his supportive presence as she gave a deeply spiritual witness of what the Gospel was saying to her.

Due to political disturbances and civil war in neighboring countries, the Diocese is home to a large number of refugees from Angola, Democratic Republic of Congo and Rwanda. These refugees are ministered by a religious community of sisters and a priest. I received a letter from Sister John Mary Mulenga, Sc.J, who works with the refugees. She says in her simple way:

Greetings from Meheba refugee camp.

I hope you are fine. Just a word to say

you gave to me and my community.

The retreat really helped me to image God

in new ways. You helped me deepen my

Spiritual life. You are a great woman of our

day. Keep it up with the same Spirit.

I miss you.

I must admit that our invitation by Bishop Kasonde to give Wholeness/Holiness Retreats to the sisters was anticipated with a feeling of assurance but the call to give the retreat to the priests was extremely unnerving. I'm ok with the women but what will I do with the men? No bishop or priest has ever called me to this walk with God with men as the retreatants. Only because I did a trust walk with my doubtful self did I agree to this walk of faith. We proceeded with our theme: Our Journey into God.

- We revisited our initial calling of Jesus to come and follow in his footsteps of service.

- We spent time exploring our images of God whose desire is to become one of us.

- We opened to one another the spiritual journeys that kept us on this pathway.

- We spent time in experiencing a variety of ways we could deepen our life of prayer.

- Blocks to our spiritual journey were identified and publicly discarded. This activity will become a daily part of how we strengthen our call to follow Jesus.

- Each person publicly renewed their vocation by deepening their promise to follow and what that will look like in the year ahead. Each person was supported by the others in their promise to support them through the year.

- The life journey of growth stages, as described by Richard Rohr, was described and examined by Bishop Kasonde and the priests together and by the sisters and the bishop.

Mass was celebrated by Bishop Kasonde with the priests and sisters. With hope in their hearts they can and will endure what lies ahead for each of them as they respond 'YES!' to God's call to follow (Trasna moments!) In the land where the Spirit moves freely and in a land which resembles the poverty of a Bethlehem manger where Jesus came to be born among us, they go onward down the path created for them by God. Their hope holds on to the God who calls, in the God who sends them forth, and who is one with all creation.

The evaluations by the priests were especially meaningful to me. Examples of their renewed spirit are shown in their phrases:

- The days have been full of meaning and inspiration.
- Our spirits were rocked.
- We were shown a more interior and deeper way of praying.
- The insights I received were soul enriching.
- Retreats of this kind need to be encouraged.
- The talks reminded me of my relationship with God by being true to my priestly identity in giving the best of myself.

- There was good participation from the participants, everyone got involved.
- The two presenters, Connie and Margie, were alive. They never sent us to sleep. They should keep up that spirit. I request that they come again next year.
- I have grown spiritually.
- This retreat was very enriching. It helped me to enliven my drooping spirit.
- I am particularly pleased with the topic on the "Awareness of God." I never think I know all.
- This was the first ever opportunity for all sisters and clergy to meet and pray together. I urge this ought to be done as often as means may allow.
- I bemoan the absence of those who could not make it to this great time.
- It was very enriching; practically spiritual.
- The time was not enough. We could have done or learned more. God bless the sisters.
- I had time to revisit my vocation.
- The image of God as Breath, whose sound is YHVH, struck me the most. My very breathing is an image of God within and an image of God being breathed forth from me.
- The facilitators have really helped me be aware of God's presence in my daily life. They have been themselves in their simplicity, openness and humility, a clear testimony of the presence of God.

When African men and women begin to formulate their spiritual journey with Jesus as a priest or sister they are given a prayer composed, by Sister Margie Hosch, OSF, as a letter from Jesus to them as follows:

Jesus Prayer for You

Live large, O my people!

My universe is huge.
All that I have created needs to be cared for.
Take a good long look at me while you pray forth your life to see
how it is done.
Let my dreams of loving large enter into your mind, into your
heart, into your very soul.
It takes everyone working together to do large loving by and for
all on earth that has life.
Remember again my words that we are all together making up
the Body of Christ.
Take a good look at me and ponder how it is to be done.
Let my Spirit, my dreams, my life, my words and my actions and
my dying enter onto your mind, into your heart and into your
very being.
You in me and I in you and we in all that has life.
Create a birthquake of love so that all may experience being
familied as one for all eternity
without end.
Become as family to provide the basic necessities of life as you
hear the cries for food, water, housing, health care, healing,
education and employment.
Hear the cries of the earth and all living creatures that have life.

It takes all people to feed the multitudes with the basic necessities of life.

Listen intently to take a soul picture of your brothers and sisters in despair, loneliness, forgotten, who are angry, lost, without purpose, abused, abusive, hopeless, orphaned, addicted and suffering of all kinds.

Preserving, caring, loving all into life after birth is the way to take up your cross and follow me.

The ripples of large loving will take caring, forgiving, listening, giving, sharing, generosity and action when you give yourself over to be my disciple.

You will come to know of my love for all that I have created. You will come to believe in my love for YOU.

Do not store into barns your gifts, your talents, your energies, your resources, but share them for the building up of all that makes up my whole created earth which exists as only a small blue marble in the ever expanding universe.

I leave no one ungifted, especially you. I am showing you the way forward.

Your extravagant loving Jesus

Let us walk humbly, in openness and simplicity, as we go forward as brothers and sisters of the world, living always in the presence of God. The poor await our blessing. We await the blessing of the poor.

On the third trip Sisters Margie and Connie conducted a Retreat for 18 Sisters and another Retreat for 17 Priests, 5 Deacons, 2 Brothers and 3 Capuchin students.

Work back home:

Returning home Sisters Connie and Margie went to work to do what they could to provide help for the poor in Zambia. The following is a sample of the work that was and is being done due to their influence:

Sister Connie asked her parish, St. John Vianney, to assist Bishop Kasonde. The parish put out the following special announcement titled, "Journey to Solwezi, Zambia" explaining how parishioners could be involved in helping the Diocese of Solwezi. (Trasna moment for all!)

Lenten Service Project
St. John Vianney Parish, Janesville, WI
"Journey to Solwezi, Zambia"

During Lent, St. John Vianney's Peace and Justice Committee is challenging you to participate in several activities that will help families living in Solwezi, Zambia.

When our parishioner, Sister Connie Fahey, went to Solwezi, Zambia in July, 2011, she had no idea of how much her heart would be touched and changed. She returned home to Janesville, grateful for having spent time with Bishop Charles Kasonde and his wonderful priests and sisters who are bringing Christianity and the Catholic Church to an area of the world where Catholicism has not been before.

These men and women have given their lives to thousands of desperately poor men, women and children of the Northern part of Zambia which is geographically almost the size of Wisconsin. The priests and sisters live and minister in the bush country where electricity, running water, and the comforts of modern society haven't reached yet. These magnanimous missionaries, who are pragmatic, fun-loving, great singers and dancers, joyfully give their life to the least of their brothers and sisters who eke out a living on the edge of the third-world society.

Walking around the teeming compounds and Solwezi streets, Sister Connie noted that the children were not in school, played with soccer balls made of plastic bags wound into balls and played in the dirt and mud that was everywhere, molding the mud into figures. And while touring the schools where the Sisters taught, she noticed that there were no books. So Bishop Kasonde was delighted when she suggested that she would go home and start collecting children's books, so that every child in his diocese would own at least one book and the schools could have a few educational books to lend out to the children.

During Lent there are a series of activities for you to participate in:

On February 25-26 and March 3-4, there will be a collection of children's books. We all have books that are gathering dust. The children of Solwezi have no books! So during the first two weeks in Lent we will be collecting gently-used children's books, books appropriate for pre-school ages through eighth grade. Select books that are wholesome books, those that you want your children or grandchildren to read, that feed and nourish their minds, hearts and spirits. There will be boxes in the Gathering Space to collect the books before or after each Mass. We are also looking for "Box Sponsors" at $60.00 each for the cost of mailing a box of books to the Bishop's office.

SISTER MARGIE HOSCH, OSF, SISTER CONNIE FAHEY, FSM,
MARY CATHERINE HARRIS, BILL HANCOCK

On Sunday, March 4th, 2-4 pm, plan to attend a pleasant afternoon at St. John Vianny listening to organ music and learning about life in Solwezi, Africa. To get through the doors for this affair, bring any one of the following: bar of soap, toothpaste, band-aids, a package of pencils or pens, or a small Dollar-store toy. These items are used as "stuffers" in the boxes of books. A free will offering will be taken which will be sent to the Bishop to support his efforts in educating young women on how to care for the health and nutrition of their children.

Little Dresses/Britches for Africa returns on Friday, March 16th, in Marian Hall. Join in the fun sewing with friends, old and new, as garments are made for the children of Solwezi. Watch the bulletin for more details.

No effort is complete without breakfast. Join us after each Mass on Sunday, March 25th. All proceeds will be sent to Bishop Kasonde to be used in subsidizing his school for street children. At the breakfast you will hear about how the school is conducted and about the children of Solwezi.

As we listen to the readings on the first Sunday of Lent, let us be reminded that we are loved by God who calls us to love our brothers and sisters, especially the poorest of the poor. May the Spirit hover over your head and heart and prompt you to hear the cry of the poor a half world away.

Chapter Six

The Light Is There!
...Help is coming

Zambia, 2012 – Sister Connie:

What words are used to describe transformational moments in one's life? Are there any words in the lexicon of any language to describe ineffable beauty, indefinable mystery, or the unfathomable courage I saw, heard and experienced as I imbibed the hidden prayer life of thirty-two Poor Clare nuns in Lusaka, Zambia? My few weeks among them fall into the category of a profound and an incomprehensible mountain-top experience.

These "poor ladies," following in the 800-year-old footsteps of their beloved foundress, Clare of Assisi, have no idea of the astonishing light of their being, as the renowned poet Hafiz says, as they went about their daily life of prayer and labor in the midst of banana trees, fruit orchards, vegetable and flower gardens, and the multitudinous numbers of trees and bushes. I wondered in my loosely translated Hafiz poem:

Do they know how beautiful they are?
I think not,
I saw great parades with wildly colorful bands

> streaming from their minds and hearts,
> carrying wonderful and secret messages
> to every corner of this world.
> I saw saints bowing in the mountains
> hundreds of miles away
> that break into light
> from their most common words.
> I wish I could show them,
> when they are lonely or in darkness,
> the Astonishing Light
> of their own Being!

In doing the work of the three retreats, my companion Sister Margie and I were totally immersed in listening to the stories and experiences of these holy women twelve hours a day. We must have set some kind of world record as we each conducted one hundred and thirty listening and coaching sessions and fifteen group experiences during the three weeks.

Their enclosed life caused me to ponder the question, "Why would thirty-two vibrant women dedicate their one, precious life to prayer, day-in and day-out, behind the walls of a cloister?" The simple answer is; Faith, hope and love and the greatest of these is LOVE. Pedro Arrupe, S.J. (General Superior of the Jesuits says):

Nothing is more practical than finding God that is, falling in love in a quite absolute, final way. What you are in love with, what seizes your imagination, will affect everything. It will decide what will get you out of bed in the morning, what you will do with your evenings, how you spend your weekends, what you read, who you know, what breaks your heart, and what amazes you with joy and gradtitude. Fall in love, stay in love, and it will decide everything.

Whether we are an enclosed monastic person or an active woman religious or a lay person attempting to live contemplatively in our chaotic world, we find common ground as we search for meaning for our life and are invited to participate in a love relationship with Holy Incomprehensible Mystery. It was our privilege and grace to accompany these extraordinarily beautiful women on their journey into Wholeness/Holiness and experience a few life-changing moments with them as they joyously danced, sang and beat drums in praise and thanksgiving to the Eternal Flow of God-With-Us.

Zambia, 2012 – Sister Margie:

For three and a half weeks we nestled into the dynamic rhythm of life with thirty-two Poor Clare Nuns and novices some distance from Lusaka, Zambia. Before the invitation was extended to us, there was a thorough discernment about the visit within the community:

Who are these Franciscan Sisters, Connie Fahey and Margie Hosch, from the United States?

Will their spirit be in harmony with ours?

Can they hear stirrings of our souls if from another culture and continent?

Is it possible to blend the vocations of the enclosed contemplative vocation with the evangelical and apostolic vocations in order to journey down the spiritual pathway together?

Are our life experiences too different to risk this journey?

Will language separate us from listening and hearing each other?

How will we manage around our enclosed parameters?

We were told that this discussion and discernment went on throughout the weavings of pros and cons until finally an invitation was sent from one continent to another. Please come!

Being one in the Body of Christ with love as the operating premise, we were enabled to fill the cracks of so many differences. Together, we embraced and held each other in the journey of renewing our commitment to follow in the footsteps of Jesus to follow in his footsteps of love for the poor and all creation.

Rising as a phoenix out of the ashes of past shortcomings was the strength and faith of their vocation story and how they came to know the call of Jesus to follow in his footsteps of love for the poor and all of creation. Their sorrow for past transgressions was expressed as each sister dramatized the release of her feelings. Seeking reconciliation was powerfully displayed by one sister who moved into the room in a shroud with a huge rock wrapped in it. She laboriously removed the rock, to symbolize the letting go of that which no longer lived within her. Imagine all the sisters, nine per group, releasing the power of grace that past failings have on them and doing this in the most unique, solemn, meaningful and touching ways. I take grace from that experience to follow their footsteps. To forgive oneself is a journey to freedom while creating a lightness of heart for loving. (Trasna moment!)

The days that followed brought forth individual magnificats, often expressed within the context of dramatic presentations, song and at times dancing to the rhythm of music from the CD, "The Poet, Romances for Cello." The sisters each proclaimed their renewed selves following the pattern of expressions of their own magnificat. Proclamations of their renewed self were expressed in poetry, haikus, dramatic readings, dance, beats of the drums and shakers and acted out in dramatic presentatations. Each sister received a blessing from their sisters as they moved together in the rhythm of the music from the CD, as a "Feather on the Breath of God."

After the three retreats were completed we were surprised with three more celebrations. The first was their special renewal of the vows liturgy following their retreat. They were dancing, drumming and singing along with the flowered branches being waved forth, as their words of daring to dance their dream of living totally in the spirit of prayer in their vowed life and within the enclosure of their monastery sanctified all present.

The next celebration brought us to a paraliturgy which follows their annual retreat. This took place outside as the sun was setting. A large wooden cross was placed next to a smoldering bonfire. The liturgy of prayers, songs and readings grew in intensity as the fire was set ablaze. The theme was centered on the image of God as Truth, Goodness and Beauty.

SISTER MARGIE HOSCH, OSF, SISTER CONNIE FAHEY, FSM,
MARY CATHERINE HARRIS, BILL HANCOCK

Then five sisters came forth to read reflections about this particular retreat experience:

It was a place of encounter,
Where we came together to find strength for our days,
Where our life orientations emerged,
Where a way forward was searched for the future,
Where each person mattered and contributed for the good of all.

It was a place of dialogue,
Where we listened to that which divides and unites us,
Where we unlocked the inner pains and divisions among us,
Where we faced the demons of our hearts and shared truths,
Where we sometimes pierced the hearts of each other but also,
Where we mended the broken cords between us.

It was a sacred place of renewal,
Where we sat close to our roots of life, that speak to us of respect and compassion,

Where we breathed fresh air in moments of weariness,
Where we found a reason to believe in nature's goodness,
Where we felt the silence of our ancestral presence that beckons
us to go on.

It was a place of celebrations,
Where we welcomed new life together,
Where we pronounced long, lasting commitments of love and
life,
Where we gave thanks for the great harvests of each season,
Where we sang and danced to the rhythm of the ancestral
drums.

It was a place of friendship,
That speaks to us of love, peace and harmony,
That speaks to us of unity and community,
That speaks to us of forgiveness and mercy,
That speaks to us of respect and compassion,
That speaks to us of beauty and gratitude.

Connie and Margie, we give thanks to you,
For the timely words spoken in friendship,
For the loving gestures, the forgiving smile,
For a profound silence that invades your whole being,
For a sense of presence that comes and overcomes.
We pray that you will continue to encounter this God of love
that is more distant than the stars and nearer than the eye.

We met with the total community to discern ways to carry on in the spirit of the retreat in the year ahead. Also, we met with the Abbess and her council as they begin to forge new pathways of leadership for the future in preparation for their Chapter in December.

We also met with the six novices for an afternoon of sharing their journeys to God and their desires for the cloistered life of the Poor Clares. Their vocation stories gave us some insight as to how the African women are brought to consider a vocation to the vowed life of a nun. We were very inspired by their stories.

Benedictions were given in multiple ways. We came away with cards of thanks, the memory of a celebration of tribal dances with costumes and a skit as they dramatized our unique mannerisms that brought us to gusts of laughter. Later, each sister was embraced for the final farewell.

Truly, the great divide of differences was crossed over as a new solidarity of the African and American sisters was shaped together in a supportive and loving oneness.

Down the walking path among the bushes and briars lived the religious community named the Daughters of the Redeemer. Sister Matilda Mwansa had picked us up at the airport and was eager for us to meet her Provincial, Sister Emelda Moomba, DOR, and the sisters living and working there.

As we walked over we noticed four little girls following us. We discovered that two of the girls were attending school but the other two were too poor to attend. Our hearts ached for them until we discovered that one of the missions of the Daughters was to provide education for four months to those children who couldn't afford public education.

The Daughter's life was described as being missioned for service to and living among the poorest of the poor. All the sisters had been afflicted with malaria because of their living conditions. Their housing is the same as the housing of the poor they are serving. One of the sisters described her work as the farmer, raising the crops and tending the animals in order to help feed and provide basic schooling to the many children who weren't able to attend school because of their impoverishment.

I asked where the children were taught. Sister Emelda pointed to a cement platform that once was the flooring of a building that was beyond repair during the rainy season. We discovered that they had few books, no pencils or tablets and no teaching materials of any kind. I mentioned that Sister Marie Therese Kalb had asked me to find a place for a Common Venture team. The sisters were elated and would have housing for the team in the month of June, 2013. This can be discussed this year in June, when my religious community gathers for our own visioning process in discerning our future.

After being treated to dinner we were asked if we would be willing to give the Wholeness/Holiness Retreat to the Daughters of the Redeemer in April/May of 2013. It would take four week-long retreats to accommodate all of the Daughters missioned throughout Zambia. We said a tentative yes because we would be giving the retreat for sisters with so little by way of means and access to spiritual reading and spiritual renewals. It is very humbling and also very inspiring to encounter such extreme giving of one's life to be used to build up the Body of Christ. Religious women are such strong, viable images of the presence of our God in the world. How can anyone say no to the pleas of the poor?

Then we were surprised with a visit from Bishop Charles Kasonde who made a special trip to meet with us. He expressed much gratitude to the Sisters of St. Francis of Dubuque, Iowa and the Franciscan Sisters of Mary for their support of our efforts in helping the Zambian people and especially the church in Solwezi Diocese.

He laughed when we talked about the box of bears that were received. With a twinkle in his eye he said he would prize the one with his name on it. He was very appreciative of the shipping of a container of hospital furnishings and equipment to supply some of the small clinics spread throughout the Solwezi Diocese. He mentioned his gratitude for the two large donations from donors that are helping to build two wells in Solwezi.

Before departing to the United States we spent two days with Sister Josephine and the sisters at Kalundu, where we had given three seminars three years ago. Shortly after arriving, we thought we would put our feet up to rest awhile before the long journey home. However, Sister Josephine Malenga made an announcement that a huge trailor truck carrying food stuffs from Canada just arrived and needed to be emptied. For the next two hours a small group of us emptied the food which would be passed out to the poor in the neighborhoods and prisons and some would be used at Kalundu for the sisters coming for classes. It brought back memories of working at Catholic Charities and filling a semi-truck full of supplies to aid the people in South America who were suffering the aftermath of a tsunami.

To sum up the experience of the retreats I use the words of the
Poor Clare Nuns in prayer.

Through the two guides you gave us:

You "called and cried out loud" to each of us using such
simple sounds and songs, which shattered our deafness.

O illusive God, in the forest into which you led us, and
through the simple pictures of trees that you placed before us,

You were radiant and resplendent, and you put flight
to our blindness.

O what a strange journey to the interior!
This journey "in which our eyes were opened and we saw"
"Our ears were unblocked and at last we heard"
O, the fragrance! The taste! The thrilling touch
that sets one's whole being on fire.

Help us to not walk away from these precious days
And let time cover all we experienced
In a dark cloud of forgiveness.

You touched us, and we are set on fire to attain the peace that
is yours.

**On their fourth trip Sisters Margie and Connie gave three
retreats to 28 Poor Clare Nuns.**

Chapter Seven

A Goal Has Been Reached

...A dream is realized as the water... flows

Zambia 2013, Sisters Margie and Connie at the Daughters of the Redeemer:

Our trip to Zambia this time was crammed full of planned activities that included six Wholeness/Holiness Retreats, preparing the little blue school house for its students, getting the Common Venture Team in place and then, as there always are, there will be the unexpected requests.

The Daughters of the Redeemer's inward pilgrimage began in early May this year. They are an indigenous Diocesan Congregation of Catholic Religious Sisters working in Zambia. Their Congregation was founded in 1969. In 2001 the Congregation was approved by Rome as a Congregation of Diocesan Rights. It is a nonprofit faith-based institution started for evangelization that has evolved. The Congregation now serves the Mt. Zion community located in the rural district of Chongwe, located about 30-km from Lusaka town.

This catchment area (community) contains three hundred thousand people, mostly farmers. Most of the working people make less than a dollar a day. The Congregation provides education services concentrated on empowering women in life skills and working with the youth in various activities to meet their needs.

The local community and the sisters have initiated construction of Redeemer Community School with the purpose of fighting illiteracy and helping to improve the standard of living. The main obstacle to the successful completion of the project is the lack of safe, clean and sufficient water supply for the school. In order to meet the school's water needs a new bore hole must be located and drilled, a pump put in place, installation of piping to a storage tank, erection of a storage tank on a support structure and pipe connections made to the school buildings. When we arrived, the project was at a standstill because neither the Congregation nor community had the financial resources to meet these needs.

Immediatly after arriving in Zambia for our fifth Wholeness/Holiness Retreat visit we realized that the little blue school house project was in dire need of additional funding and sent the following letter back to our supporters in the United States:

Dear Friends,

When we arrived in Lusaka at the Daughters of the Redeemer motherhouse we were informed that the Daughters are in the process of building a small school for local children who do not have access to school because they are too poor. They have built the small four-room school to teach basic English, mathematics and reading. The school has been funded by donations from business, grants, government and other donors. Because there is not enough money to provide water and toilet facilities, we are *petitioning our friends to help the sisters put water and toilet facilities into this building. This project will cost around $18,500. In addition, we also know, that the 500 children coming into this small school will not have had a decent meal before walking one to three miles to attend school. The sisters do not have funds to provide a small snack to the children.*

Therefore, we are making an urgent appeal to you to help them. The Sisters of St. Francis Common Venture Program is providing the services of five sisters and four lay teachers to assist the Daughters in teaching the children for the month of June. It would be nice if the Team has access to toilet facilities and water on the premises rather than having to walk back to their residence, about half a mile at the motherhouse. The need is urgent and the water could be put in immediately if you make a donation toward this

project in the next week or two.
Sisters Margie and Connie Report Progress to Donors:

Three years ago the Daughters of the Redeemer made a commitment to the people of the Mt. Zion community to provide education for impoverished families surrounding their farm, Formation House and Retreat House. The Daughters surveyed the area and discovered that there are over five hundred children who are unable to go to school because they are either too poor or it is too far for them to walk to the public school located at a great distance from the area.

The sisters approached the civic community, parents and businesses and wrote grants to entities in Spain and Holland to finance the building of a little school. From the monies received they have begun building a little four-room school that can accommodate the children by offering classes in three shifts a day beginning in the month of June.

Because of the limited funds they were unable to connect electric power and provide water to the school's bathrooms and drinking water for the children. Upon arriving in Zambia, we observed the progress of the building and what was still needed for the completion of the school. This prompted us to e-mail you asking for monies for the water system.

We investigated what it would cost when we spoke with the Bishop of Solwezi who has installed various types of water systems in his diocese. If a simple pump and spigot is placed in the middle of a village, the cost is around $6,000 like the one built and we blessed while in Solwezi.

Bishop Kasonde said connecting water to the school and latrine would cost at minimum $18,000 which includes surveying the area for its water table, drilling a bore hole, purchasing and installing pipes to transport the water half a mile from the bore hole to a holding tank, purchasing the retention tank and installing a rack to hold the retention tank. Transportation costs of getting machinery to the rural site to drill and install pipes are an additional cost. To date, $12,000 has been donated. When people's hearts are moved to compassion for the poor, miracles happen. This is what you accomplished in little over three weeks.

The other miracle was finding a water table. The first surveyor informed the sisters that there was no possibility of water near enough to the school. Sister Brenda, in charge of the project, didn't give up. She trusted the project was in the hands of God. She proceeded to hire a second surveyor who searched and searched and finally discovered not only a water table but two streams of water converging at the foot of the hill upon which the little school is perched. When the family of God works together to stand with the poor, no obstacle is too great to make way for a miracle. Needless to say, we all gathered in a dance of celebration.

The next miracle required was to install a ceiling in the school, connect the electrical power to the building, provide school supplies and get furnishings for the school. Are we dreaming too big for small children who walk miles to obtain an education only available to them if this little blue school in the bush exists? We might be, but we choose to dream along with the Daughters of the Redeemer and our wondrous donors.

We are wading deeper and deeper into the culture of Zambian women who share their lives with us in the Wholeness/Holiness Retreats. These women share their stories, faith and their experiences of ministries among vulnerable children, women and those who live on the margins of Zambian society. After completing two retreats, we were introduced to their various ministries both near and far from their motherhouse in Lusaka.

Stories we have only read about become our firsthand experience. From Lusaka we drove on a rutted, potholed road into the bush to visit a Daughters of the Redeemer ministry in the village of Chibomo. The ministry there is for teenage and older mothers who have had no opportunity to learn to read and write. To address the needs of these women, the sisters hold a class on Monday, Wednesday and Friday in a covered, dilapidated shelter that has no classroom furnishings or school supplies for teaching and learning. All the women sit on the dirty floor, while the instructor teaches them a few basic concepts of math and pronunciations of English and the Chibomo native languages of Lenje and Bemba.

The women were not distracted by our presence among and observing them. They were intent on learning the languages so that they will be able to read and write all three of them. After the class when we said we were proud of them, they all laughed and clapped their hands. They are a beautiful people!Another ministry

the sisters are implementing for single mothers in this village is a community gardening project on their convent plot of land. This has been a wonderful way to introduce these very young women to an employable skill that will support them and their children. But the biggest problem in making this a successful ministry is the lack of water. The sisters have access to the village water source but they must pay for every drop used from the small spigot owned by the village. The village leaders turn the water on for only two hours in the morning and two hours in the late afternoon, so water is scarce even if it seems to be available.

Women walk from great distances to the villiage to get water for their gardens and other uses. They carry the water away in gallon containers and store it. The Daughters keep buckets of water in their home for cleaning, bathroom and washing uses. They are constantly using their ingenuity to get water for the needs of the women and themselves. After returning from this trip, we were exhausted. As a result we had to cancel another trip into the bush. The trip would have been to a site where the Daughters have been given a plot of land to build a boarding school for girls. That kind of school is needed in that area because girls who walk to school are subject to capture by people involved in trafficking. The captured girls are sent to South Africa and then on to multiple nations of the world, including America.

Therefore, young girls in this part of Zambia cannot be educated safely without having a safe haven like the boarding school the Daughters want to provide. However the needs are so overwhelming and the costs so beyond the Daughters' financial capability that the sisters are struggling to find a way to begin this project. Wouldn't it be great to find a movie star, philanthropic organization, religious group or a multinational business that wants to take up this cause? One can dream, right?

The day to drill the bore hole had come! It was the day of promise as we gathered at the site where water was discovered. All was ready for the bore hole to be dug. Pictures were taken as we rejoiced with the possibility of supplying the little blue schoolhouse with water. One hour passed as the drill ground out the mountain rock. No water yet!

Two hours passed as the mound of drilled dirt kept growing. No water yet! Young boys were sent to bring down folding chairs for us to sit and rest our tired legs. The third hour of drilling brought the once exuberant sisters to a worried stance. No water yet! The fourth hour brought skepticism, anxious countenance, and

silent cries of dashed hopes. As the drill ground down 65, 70 and finally 75 meters deep, the drill manager, without words, gave the desultory signal of NO WATER! And the drilling stopped.

Where there had been hope, now despair! Where there had been light, now darkness! Where there had been high expectations, now nothing! The silent cries of the gathered resounded in broken hearts. A dirge-like procession of sisters climbed the hill toward home. No words could be found to describe the depth of a broken dream of water for the impoverished children soon coming to begin the school year. Mourning could not be stilled by tender embraces and condolences of love. We were one with the Psalmist: *my strength is broken as a shard of pottery, and my mouth is dry; You have laid me in the dust of the bushes...* (Ps 22 adapted from Psalms for Praying, Nan Merrill)

A few hours later, a ringing of the phone pierced the silence. The school building contractor called to say, "Come to the hole!" We dropped everything and came running to the site of the unproductive bore hole. As we gathered with perplexed questioning, the school contractor proceeded to drop a rock into the hole. The echo of a stone resounded in our unbelieving ears as we heard it plunge into the water's depth. His words are still ringing, "There is water in the hole!"

A phone call was made to the geologist to ascertain the viability of the bore hole. He said he would come the next day to verify the findings. Despair turned to hope! Darkness turned to light! Nothing became something!

With growing faith, the following morning was spent in prayer at the site of the bore hole. If Moses could get water out of a rock, so can women of faith expect a miracle that a once dry bore hole could produce enough water to flow from the hole to the school.

The next afternoon the geologist called the sisters to the site where he was examining a second bore hole that was dug fifteen years ago and was declared dry. With glee in his voice, "You not only have a new producing bore hole, but you have water rising in this old bore hole as well." The water had risen from nowhere to 14 meters to the top of the old bore hole and 13 meters to the top of the new bore hole. Having made the holy hour at the newly dug well early that morning, we were rejoicing that possibly Moses was not the only one who could draw water from a rock. Those having gathered who had only dry tears were now crying wet tears of renewed faith in our loving God.

The Little Blue School Coming to Life Right before Our Eyes!

When the journey seems long, when we become discouraged along the way,

You restore us with Living Waters.

Bless our tears of rejoicing that flow like a stream
running to meet the Living Waters of Your Love.

May you hold us in the highs and lows
of our lives from this time forth and forevermore.

You are the Love of our life!

When the Divine Lover enters our human heart
all our yearnings are fulfilled.

May all the donors who have honored us with their gifts of financial resources rejoice along with us in ever deepening faith in the reality that we are all one in the Body of Christ wherever we happen to be born. Thank you for your trust for giving without seeing. We walk with you in faith and trust because you gave your resources to our poor brothers and sisters without counting the cost. As Jesus said, "The poor will always be with you." We open our eyes with you to see their dry tears here in the bush of Mt. Zion, Zambia, where the Daughters of the Redeemer give their total life begging for those on the farthest edges of our sight. This is the road less traveled by most of us.

Next, we celebrated Pentecost on Mt. Zion. The Spirit is eternally searching for a foothold in the swirling sands of the hills and valleys surrounding Mt. Zion. It takes persevering faithfulness to catch the wind of Spirit. The Daughters of the Redeemer have responded to the call to give away life to receive life. When hearts are saturated with energies of love, outpoured energy is reawakened for even more love and service. The relentless wind of Mt. Zion is an ever present sacrament of Spirit-power which inspirits tired and exhausted souls often spent by loving-service fatigue.

The rising dawn of Pentecost began with the experience of no water yet to be piped into the faucets and showers of the new school. This came as no surprise since we are now well adapted to the realities of no electricity and water. On our way to Mass on this morning we started on the journey over dusty, grassy and sometimes rocky pathway winding through the bush, keeping an eye out for unbidden creatures underfoot. As we walked along, we came atop a roadblock where a tree limb was felled on our pathway. Undaunted, we lifted it to the side and continued on toward our destination of celebrating liturgy with the Poor Clare nuns and the worshipping community who live within the bush.

One with those who were gathered to celebrate Pentecost with the Poor Clares, our worship experience opened with a haunting melody invoking the Spirit's presence among us in the local language of Nyanja. The Poor Clare nuns dramatized the descent of the Spirit through a powerful dance, drumming and song. Throughout the liturgy, flower branches were waved in summoning the Spirit. As the Alleluia was sung softly by the congregation the Spirit was invoked in multiple launguages of Bemba, Nyanja, English, Yonga, Lozi, Lunda, Luvale and Kaonde.

The homily reiterated that the Spirit of Pentecost is about the gathering of all the world into the Body of Christ. Every child, woman and man is equal in this Body of Christ. Ministry in Zambia is less about life after death but more about life after birth. Looking into a child's pleading eyes in need of belonging, the Spirit offers the promise that they are loved and that they will always have a place in the family of God.

Our prayers rise like incense to the Spirit awaking us to the all-encompassing presence of everyone in the family of God regardless of our being different from one another in multiple ways. We walked home in an ever-deeper realization that nothing can separate us from the love of God, wherever we may happen to be if we believe that we are united in the power of the Spirit.

We are about to embark on our fifth retreat beginning this evening at 7 pm. The retreat participants who just finished a retreat on Saturday buoyed us up by their gracious thank you in these following remarks:

- We thank your religious communities and all who have supported you to reach us and make this retreat fruitful.

- As a result of your generosity of heart, we are a "Sunrise Circle" that will continue to shine for the people we serve.

As we write, some young men are completing the trenches for the pipes to be laid tomorrow. Those pipes will bring water from the holding tank near the foundation house to the tank on the newly-built frame near the school. There are still multiple tasks to be finished at the school before it meets the Education Department's approval. The Common Venture Team may be teaching on the hillside like Jesus did but we are not sure about how to multply food for the children.

After the retreats are over, the Daughters are anxious to put the Common Venture Team members' names on their bedroom doors and give them a big welcome. The team may be elicited to help with the move into the school the first few days after they arrive here. However, hope holds that all will be ready before the team arrives. The four lay teachers who will be teaching in the school will be assigned upon completion of the building. Progress seems to move very slowly here in the Zambian bush. Nothing is simple here.

Our final retreat was a special one given to four women who are in formation along with their formators. One of the women in formation said, "I especially liked spending two days with the formation directors and all in formation with me. We went deeper into the commitment of living the four principles upon which our life is founded. We increased our communication skills so we can express our feelings to one another and be more open with each other. We role-played with our directors and learned how to speak assertively rather than aggressively or submissively. Spiritually, I am ready to commit my life to serve with the Daughters of the Redeemer."

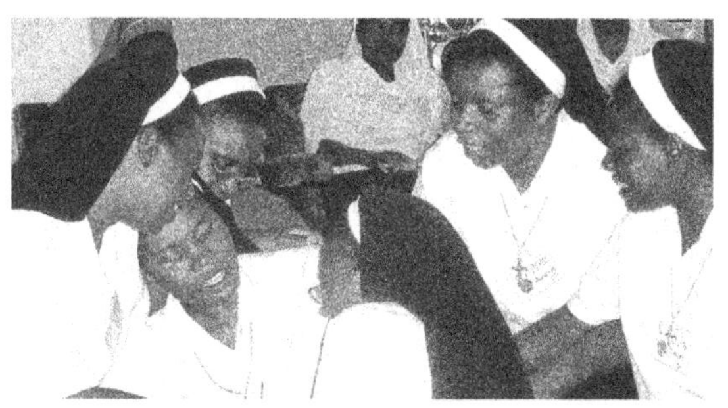

The retreat ended with laying hands on each other as we prayed for a gift of the Spirit to strengthen them for their journey.

Each of the six retreat groups had its own rhythms of dancing, singing and praising God. The drums beat out the rhythms of their African spirit of life. The songs sung in many vernacular languages told their stories. Our spirits were bathed in the rhythms of their dancing and singing. We entered into their joyous ways of praising Father, Son and Spirit as we celebrated Pentecost and Trinity Sunday.

A note was delivered from the diosese office to Sr. Connie and Sr. Margie. It stated that the Common Venture Team sent by Franciscan Common Venture, a volunteer service program administered by the Sisters of St. Francis in Dubuque, Iowa, left on schedule and will arrive Friday morning. The team members who will be assisting Sr. Connie and Sr. Margie at the new school are Sr. Carole Freking, Georgy Kurtzhals, Patti Jackson, Carrie Campbell, Sr. Phyllis Vaske, Sarah Hummelgard and Sr. Janet Kreber.

A very dedicated, excited but tired Common Venture Team arrived at Lusaka, Airport on Friday, May 31st. Sisters Connie and Margie, along with five Daughters of the Redeemer, greeted them as they came through customs into the airport lobby. On Saturday the team recovered from flying 22 hours half-way around the world. Then on Sunday, they attended a celebratory welcoming dinner at the Daughters of the Redeemer's Generalate in Lusaka. Twenty Daughters from the surrounding area and their Mother Superior welcomed the Team.

On opening day of the little blue school the Team members stood at the door greeting the children as they entered. One wide-eyed young fellow stopped and looked at the ladies and said, "Are they my teachers? They look different from me."

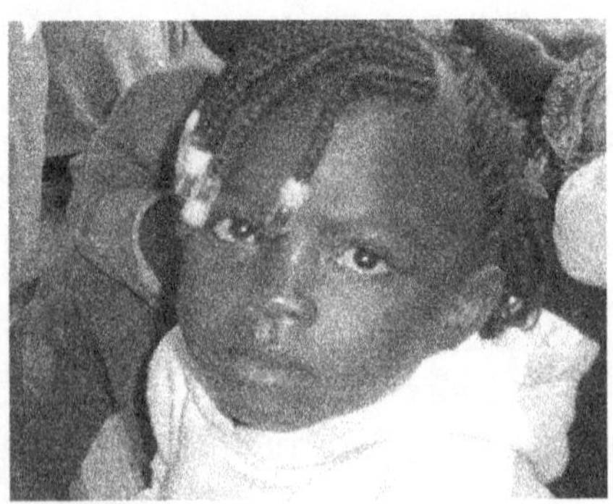

Sisters Margie's and Connie's reflections back home:

The rising sun on Mount Zion, the Daughters of the Redeemer's formation house, spoke to us as we sojourned each morning for three months with the Daughters, Fathers, Brothers and the Common Venture Team to celebrate and receive our spiritual life of Communion in and for the Body of Christ. What grace etched our souls as we were plunged into the oneness of us all. The illusion of separateness was beginning to wane. Possessions were only important if they aided the hungry, thirsty, and sick of those who live in the bush and become known to us. Education and financial gifts were begged for and given to build up the Body of Christ by meeting their very basic needs. Encountering another out of our prism of abundance called us to ask for help for the Daughters who give life out of a prism of scarcity. Truly a very special bond was created by those who rose to the occasion to share of their financial means.

As our eyesight begins to fade in our aging years, our souls often take over and see for us. We see the disparity between the gates of greed and the pathways of the heart that lead to a global embrace of love by the sharing of our spiritual and material resources with all who have been given life. Each person has many gifts. And to what purpose do we have them? Our hearts throb with renewed energies to unite with all who have the imagination, the drive and the vision to bridge the great chasm between the realities that separate us from each other.

Franciscan Sister Ilia Delio poses this question. *"What is the dream of the human family that longs to be fulfilled through the giving of your life?"* Our lives are to be lived out of the depth of this question as individuals and communities respond to the voices of the world crying out for assistance of all kinds. This question presumes that our talents, gifts, financial resources, our imagination and dreams, our experience of life and our collaboration efforts will be given.

With opened eyes and hearts we knew that what we have is for the good of all the people of Lusaka and Solwezi, Zambia. This became visible to us as the destitute people walked out of the bush needing food, education, medicines, water and safety. We embraced these people with loving responses resulting in a school being built; education for children and mothers made available; a fresh water well was dug; our sisters in Christ, The Daughters of the Redeemer, were renewed in spirit through their retreat experiences; shoes and clothing for children and their mothers; lunches were shared with children who had nothing to eat. The spirits of the Common Venture Team were renewed in their giving of time, talent, love and care to needy children.

Our sacred donors are living out the reality of joining with a global community that is collaborating in focusing generous financial resources to relieve the privation experienced by the people living in the Zambian bush. Much is needed just to ameliorate the stark needs, no less over come them, but hope is being fed by a sense that the growing concern of caring people is concentrating on the needs of the people living in and coming out of the bush.

We pose the question: How do we as church, religious communities of women and men, parishes, businesses, organizations and families join together to address global issues of poverty, hunger, thirst, human trafficking of young women, AIDS, malaria, the scarcity of education, lack of transportation and the struggling efforts of women religious to provide clinics in isolated areas?

We are hearing prophetic challenges coming from multiple voices in church and society. They are inviting each community, family, organization, church and business to bring their five loaves and two fish to be multiplied in order to address the sin-story of poverty, hunger, thirst, human trafficking, destruction of the earth, wars and violence and the insignificance and sterility at times of institutional separateness from human needs. The 'sound of no sound' is shrill when the 'no sound' is coming from populations of destitution without means of communicating their plight to the world. It takes communities willing to work together to locate these populations, to hear their sounds of dire impoverishment previously squelched into silence. We are a world family sent by God to hear the silent speak.

The 'sound of no sound' resounds when the voices of our theologians and philosophers try to explain how we are "an image of God." As we read and study the learnings of the new cosmology, we may begin to have an inkling of what it means that the millions upon billions of cells in our bodies are imprinted with God's image. Every cell in our body is connected to a Transcendent Divine essence. Every other person on this planet earth is a carrier of this same Divine imprint.

We are connected to each other no matter where we live in this world. We are connected as being "Present to the Presence" and "Presence to the Present." We come from God, we belong to God, and we are dependent upon God. St. Francis lived out of this reality. Brother Sun, Sister Moon, and Sister Water were embraced as family.

When the Divine in you connects with the Divine in me, we are physically, emotionally and spiritually inhaling and exhaling

Divine Love's energy. Because this Trinitarian Love Dance is the energy which gives life and breath to every cell, atom, proton, and boson in the human and cosmic family of God, we exhale and inhale this Divine Love Breath. God is of our very breath. To deny this oneness and live only for our individual sense of happiness and fulfillment is to drop out of the cosmic dance and live the 'illusion of separateness'.

The 'illusion of separateness' is too small for a global sojourner. What we are willing to do together will change creation forever. Let the communion story of oneness evolve. The 'sound of no sound' is becoming audible for those who are 'bonded by being'.

On their fifth trip Sisters Margie and Connie conducted six Wholeness/Holiness Retreats, welcomed the members of the Common Venture Team and joined with them in opening a school.

Chapter Eight
New Eyes See Privation and Hope
… Another hears the call and makes a choice

Mary Catherine's Invitation:

"Are you sitting down?"

This question, when it comes from the other side of a phone conversation, almost always suggests there's a surprise in store. When it was posed for me by Sister Margie Hosch in a phone call early December, 2013, I laughed, as the tone of her voice gave no hint of anything dreadful. I also knew it was likely nothing frivolous, but I had no clue what was on her mind.

Yes, I was sitting down and it's a good thing because her next question was, "Would you consider going with me to Zambia?"

I remember her words better than mine, for I think I may have responded with babble that went on for a couple of minutes: "What!....Margie!...."Well, Sure!"...."I Mean, I Don't Know!...."Are You Serious?" (While thinking, "Have you lost your mind?")

I have not lived a sheltered life, but neither had I ever traveled outside the United States. Additionally, I understood this invitation to mean I would be teaming with Margie to give the Wholeness/ Holiness Retreats to women religious! Seriously? Margie has years of experience as a certified counselor, and her focus is the psychological part of the retreats, while mine has been the spiritual component. Interesting in itself that this dedicated sister trusts a laywoman with the spiritual part of a retreat she developed and has given for years. I would say there is a little "letting go" in that.

This lay woman, a novice in retreat work, more comfortable in participating than in leading a retreat, was being asked to slip into a slot that had been filled previously on five trips to Zambia by Sister Connie Fahey. I had never met Connie, except through Margie, and that was enough to let me know that Connie's were no shoes I could fill. These thoughts and more were bumping against one another and mingling in my mind. But within all the mix, I knew my answer was, "Yes!" It seemed the answer had been in place prior to the question, but if I did truly have any say, it would be, "Yes!" (Trasna moment!)

As I prepared to say, "I want to talk to my daughters," the words never left my tongue because, as if reading my mind in that moment, Margie said, "I want to talk to your daughters. I want to help them to understand what this could be like for you, to know you will be safe." We ended the conversation with my intention to contact my children, but I knew what their responses would be and I could already envision myself on the way to Zambia.

The following morning, I e-mailed Karen, Lisa and Jan and like little ducks in a row, they came back with, "Yes!" "Yes!" "Yes!" Of course, as time went on, the reality of their mother, who was fast becoming their child, being on the continent of Africa for six and a half weeks began to sink in with a little anxiety.

Christmas-giving that year was themed for the trip, new lighter-weight luggage and various accoutrements for travel. All things considered, my children and grandchildren were, "all in" and excited. My two brothers were, "in", as well, but perhaps a little less so. Having initially affirmed the experience and never really backing down from that, there was a little stronger hint of anxiety in conversations with them. I remember one phone conversation during which my brother Ed said, "I am not sure how I feel about this." I think that meant he felt unsure, though he would not have considered discouraging me from going.

The time between Margie's phone call and our date of departure was filled with getting a passport for the first time in my close to 69 years of life; getting the okay from my doctor, along with a regimen of vaccinations; making travel arrangements to take us from Raleigh-Durham International Airport an hour from my home to the airport in Lusaka, Zambia more than an ocean away. Then there was preparing for three weeks of retreat with some 25 women, making Zambia and travel-friendly wardrobe purchases and continuing to juggle other responsibilities at home. In all the busyness, there was the continual desire to step aside and just be present to the One who with me was orchestrating all that was happening in my life.

I was about two-thirds of the way through a course of training in spiritual direction and grateful for the part of the process I had gleaned. At the same time, I was wishing to have more understanding and experience in this area as I prepared to embark on this mission of spiritually companioning others. My instructors were excited for the opportunity the Zambian experience would afford me and saw it as a practicum of sorts, monitored by Margie. It seemed that every piece of the puzzle was fitting into place for the "rightness" of this missional adventure.

My church received a special offering for our trip, wanting to provide for needs we may encounter among the people of Zambia and for any personal needs that may arise. A special commissioning service was offered the Sunday before we departed.

My children gathered in my home on that Sunday and invited extended family and friends to come for a send-off celebration. It was a fun and carefree gathering; it was also a time of checking out this person who had asked me to accompany her to Zambia. My daughters had met Margie and what they had experienced with her made them comfortable. They also knew the impact she had had on my personal journey. As my brothers and others close to me met Margie, they were taken in by her spirit and it seems everyone left that day feeling more at ease.

Filled with the joy and affirmation of that gathering so brimming with love and with a certainty of the calling to this time and place, I was ready to fly to Lusaka, Zambia. I was no longer sitting down. With the love and support of my family and friends, trust in Sister Margie Hosch, confidence in my calling to this time and place and trust in the One who calls, I never second-guessed the decision to go to Zambia. (Trasna moment!)

Margie and I left from Raleigh-Durham International on a Wednesday for Boston on the first leg of our trip to Lusaka, Zambia. In a sense, it was comforting to have a stop in our homeland before boarding another flight that would take us across the Atlantic to Amsterdam.

How awesome it was as we left Boston to peer out the window and know we were truly on our way! Amazingly, even the increased vulnerability of flying over a huge body of water did not unsettle me. The feeling was akin to what I had experienced when I felt so right and free in the moment that the risk was hardly an issue.

A few moments into the flight, Margie looked inside her bag for some item and pulled out three pieces of paper she did not recognize. These turned out to be notes from my daughters which Jan had slipped in as she had taken us to the airport earlier that day. I knew immediately that my girls were remembering notes I had tucked into their lunchboxes for school and they were wanting to provide the same for this mom/child. I also knew Margie was ready for these gestures to come to a close. They seemed to magnify her sense of responsibility for taking this beloved woman away from her beloved family.

In truth, Margie did not take me away. She was simply the channel through which the call and lure were delivered. I chose to go away. I chose to go to this place to give myself, where unbeknownst to me, I would find more of myself and a bit more of home.

Landing in Amsterdam early the following morning and a few time zones ahead of home, provided my first experience of going through customs, which was relatively and thankfully uneventful. We were relieved to land on time, as our schedule allowed only a couple of hours before the flight to Lusaka. We focused on finding the gate for this next flight, that would be a little more than twelve hours. Then we were content to sit out the waiting time.

The KLM flight we boarded to fly to Africa was unusually comfortable and accommodating. Yet there were hours upon hours to while away, and we spent a substantial part of that time playing a simple card game which Margie knew, Up and Down the River. We went up and down that river playing cards many times and up and down the aisle stretching our legs a few times while flying over land and sea to Lusaka. And we talked and talked and talked about what was ahead.

I am not certain when the sneezing and coughing started, but somewhere along the way from North Carolina to Africa, the ground work was laid for a miserable first few hours in our new location.

Mary Catherine's Initial Reflections in Zambia:

We landed in Lusaka a little before 11:00 p.m. in a light rain in the last month of the rainy season. As I stepped onto African soil to walk from the plane to the terminal, I looked up at the cloud-filled sky and knew there was a moon I could not see. The same moon I gaze upon from my own backyard and the same moon my family and friends would be viewing just a few hours later than I during my stay in Zambia. That was a comfort in this land new to me but also, I was reminded, now part of me.

We were in and out of the airport in minutes, thanks to friendly immigration officials and the two women who came to meet us, whose international community of Comboni Missionary Sisters, had invited and would host us. My first surprise was that these two women were not African. Sister Kandy and Sister Chuy, both born in Mexico, took hold of our baggage and led us out into the African night time air and to their vehicle.

The vehicle, right away, reminded me that we were away from home. I was as offered the front seat and the door I opened, as I would on one of our cars, was not the passenger's door but the driver's. Then when the vehicle pulled onto the road, the driver turned to travel in the left lane rather than the right, the British influence.

Unfamiliar as they were to me, these aspects of driving were minimal compared to the extraordinary adventures which lay ahead on our road trips in Zambia. The proverbial "washboard" does not come close to describing the roads. I've never been whitewater rafting, but I think it must feel something like the roads in Zambia, perhaps without water. You would not believe how many ruts and potholes can be crammed into one kilometer of distance. Cruising on even pavement like the worst road in Warren County where I live would be a rare and welcome surprise here in Zambia.

Arriving at the Comboni Sisters' compound on the edge of Lusaka, we stopped before two solid metal gates, locked and connected to a high concrete wall. I took note of the jagged fragments of glass embedded on top. Entering, I learned there was a dog, penned during the day and released at night to patrol. After we unloaded our baggage, the vehicle was parked in a padlocked garage. I took a deep breath. Realizing I was secure where we were, my antennae also instantly rose.

Ironically, during our entire six-and-a-half weeks stay, there was not one moment when I felt unsafe. We stayed with the Comboni Sisters and in five additional places overnight. We made day visits to two religious communities. We walked through missions and clinics, markets and villages out among the people. We traveled through an animal park and spent hours on many roadways and one waterway. We were vulnersble, yet I felt safe!

Almost immediately upon arriving I came down with a cold-symptom illness that kept me in bed for the first day in Zambia. With all the medications we took and the vaccinations received before traveling, it seems we were lacking in anything for a common cold, if there is really anything. I had some mega doses of vitamin C, which I should have started taking before we departed. Sister Margie and Sister Giuliana, one of the Comboni Sisters, doctored me with hot water flavored with lemon, from trees on the property, and sugar. Margie, ten years older than I, braved the elements and was running around taking care of me. No surprise, as her energy and stamina are amazing.

We were advised to eat nothing raw, except fruits we peeled ourselves, to avoid milk and seafood and drink only water that had been boiled. During the first days, I found myself unthinkingly going for some lettuce to make a salad. Thankfully, Margie intercepted that move.

Usually, our meals were prepared by one or more of the sisters in whatever community we were visiting, sometimes with the help of laywomen in the local village. When we were with the Franciscan Sisters of Assisi, the novices helped with the cooking. In every place, attention was given to offering foods our systems could tolerate. There was usually a pot of ground nuts, peanuts, boiling outside on a charcoal fire each day.

Breakfast was typically toasted bread with jam and/or oatmeal, which they called porridge. Lunch and supper consisted usually of an assortment of vegetables including cabbage and other varieties of leafy greens, green beans, peas, carrots, tomatoes, potatoes, sweet potatoes, rice and maize. We had chicken often and our last meal there was rabbit. Cookies were often served and sometimes cake. Ice cream was a special treat. Also, we had stashed several dozen nutrition bars and candy in our suitcases so they were also a special treat.

The staple in Zambian meals is nshima, a finely ground maize mixed with water and boiled to make a mash. I mistook it for mashed potatoes the first time it was served. The custom is to take a small "blob" with the fingers and form it into a ball, usually with one hand, then dip it into gravy or combine it with a bit of vegetable and pop it into the mouth. The people eat with their hands mostly but they provided us with silverware. All in all, we fared well, considering all the potential for illness at almost every turn.

After a short period in the company of the women in the Comboni community, I knew that I was surrounded by those who had let go in order to follow their calling to life in ministry. (Trasna moments!)

There is my travel companion, Sister Margie. For sixty years, her service has taken her into classrooms, parishes, counseling sessions, management of charities and most recently into retreat work aimed at empowering people to live and live fully and truly. She sees the world as her family and her commitment to life for all is mirrored again and again in those who minister in Zambia.

Sister Kandy, leader of the Comboni Sisters, with her sharp eyes, quick mind and compassionate heart is so in tune with the poor. Her countenance beams in their presence, as does theirs when she walks or rides through their neighborhoods. Caring for the poor and engaging in projects to give them life is routine but also life-giving for her.

Sister Lali, from Spain, is immeasurably gifted and creative, devoted to her calling, which she defines as, "to live my life for others." Lali is thirty-four years old. She works with more than 30 families in Mother Earth Project, where they grow Moringa trees, gathering and drying the leaves to make a nutritional supplement and also a healing ointment. These products improve life and also make a profit for the Comboni Sisters' ministry.

(Moringa leaf is best-known as an excellent food source of nutrition and a natural energy booster. This energy boost is not based on sugar, and so it is sustained. Moringa is also soothing. It helps lower blood pressure and is a sleep aid. Its detoxifying effect may come from Moringa's ability to purify water. Moringa acts as a coagulant attaching itself to harmful material and bacteria. It is believed that this process is taking place in the body as well.)

Mother Earth sisters take turns, two by two, living among the people, in a one-room house, without electricity and with the inside space mostly taken up by two tents which protect them from mosquitoes while sleeping. Water, drawn from a nearby well, is heated by the sun for bathing. Water for drinking is boiled from the heat of a simple charcoal burner outside in what may be called their "living" space.

Italian Sister Albertina, well into her 80's, wears sandals that have walked the neighborhoods until they seem molded to her feet. Albertina helps with a preschool, brings older children for tutoring, engages sponsors for students to attend boarding school and counsels their families. She is rarely still or alone. Her greatest challenge of tutoring is probably trying to teach us to speak her Italian version of English.

The Comboni Sisters provide hope for the people in the communities that they serve. Otherwise, the people would have little means of rising from their circumstances. The sisters provide spiritual nourshment, as well as water, food, housing, clothing, medical care, counseling, education, empowerment for living and making a living. Every waking moment for these women who minister is a moment of intention for the poor or responding to the needs of the poor.

My first experience among the people of Zambia was on Palm Sunday. We attended Mass in a poor parish in Lusaka, where my first tears came as I watched these people with next to nothing process down the aisle with such joy to place their offerings at the altar. Their fists appeared to clinch a coin or two and I was reminded of how tight-fisted we can be in our plenty.

After the church service we gathered in a huge field with people from all denominations across Lusaka. Margie and I were a bit of a spectacle, as you might imagine, and the people seemed eager to meet us. They could not have been more respectful. They came to us with outstretched hands and warm greetings, their smiles reflecting generous spirits and also the absence of dental and other health care. They spoke English, but mostly they spoke with a motion, hands together, which is their repeated expression of respect and honor.

There was a brief program on the field, followed by a procession, with what seemed like thousands of people waving palm branches and singing "Hosanna," as we walked through a poor, poor village in the city that displayed the most dire poverty imaginable. Walking in poverty is different from reading about it or seeing pictures. Particularly memorable were two sisters who were sharing one pair of shoes, one wearing the left and one, the right shoe, over-sized and over-worn.

It felt to me as if I must be walking on the suffering face and heart of Christ, and I knew in that experience there was a reason I was suffering at witnessing it. The question and call for me is, "How do I respond to what I have noticed?"

We walked past little shacks, one on top of the other, with people everywhere waving joyfully. We helped one another jump over deep ruts and step over garbage and sewage. There was a spirit of community and home. With no break from the bleakness of the physical surroundings, there was at the same time a continuous and abundant flow of beautful and joyous spirit.

At the beginning of the walk, one little girl had slipped her hand into mine and held on throughout. As the walk ended and the time came to separate, we questioned an adult in our group about what would happen to the little girl. We were assured,

"Don't worry, the people will take care of her." It seems everyone is family and home is everywhere.

These are people whose life is determined largely by the place and circumstances of their birth, for them and for us, unmerited, undeserved. This is the realization that calls and moves us, in Zambia or next door or wherever: we who have share with those who have not.

Occasionally, we rode through areas of Lusaka where we could almost forget that we were not in America. The streets were paved with curbs, well-lit and tree-lined. There were office buildings, restaurants, shops and shopping malls and homes that suggest affluence. There were adults dressed professionally talking on cell phones and children wearing uniforms, carrying backpacks, walking to and from school. But these areas are far from the norm in Zambia.

Being among these people, in this place away from our home, I was aware from the outset that we are not alone in the journey. There is a sense of Divine Presence and Spirit, and there is a sense of connection to the spirits of others, to those we met and those at home while we were there. We are accompanied and connected by one another's spirits.

We touched people, sometimes their skin, but not always their skin and not just their skin. We touched these people and we were touched by them. The question for me is, "How do I respond to what I experienced?" Looking closer at the people, what do I see? There were women with babies tied to their backs while they swept their yards or marketed their vegetables. Others walked the dusty roads with a sack of food or bucket of water balanced on their heads.

Then there were the men who weaved in and out of traffic while trying to sell everything from phone cards to Bermuda shorts. Others rode bicycles while pulling loads of wood or charcoal or they paddled canoes searching for fish to eat or sell. Some were lucky to work the few jobs available in the copper mine or on road construction.

The children were everywhere, some whose dark skin only peeked through layers of dust and dirt. There were some who slipped up quietly from behind and risked just a fingertip touch of our skin. Others have had their childhood ripped away and have been exploited into motherhood. Almost all of them loved to pose for the camera and then to see their pictures. These children's wide eyes of longing reach deep into your heart and soul.

Palm Sunday was definitely the landmark experience for me and I continue to search for and try to uncover meaning in that, in addition to recognizing the need and call to address the poverty there. For days following Palm Sunday, I could hardly speak for tears that continued to come from everywhere, it seemed. I remember Margie coming into my bedroom the next morning and finding me sitting on my bed drenched in sorrow that had entered on the Palm Sunday procession. She was a compassionate presence for me, within the deep compassion she has for anyone who suffers in any way.

Reflections of Sister Margie and Mary Catherine – Zambia 2014

Holy Week was interwoven into our first powerful retreat with eight Comboni Sisters. The days flew by as we sang and danced, cried and laughed, and prayed our faith journey behind and before us. One touching moment found us gathered in a ritual of casting away blocks which kept us from surrendering to fully taking up our cross and following Jesus. Props which helped us celebrate our newness were drumming, singing, dancing, sharing deeply, active listening, nurturing, healing, creating songs, art and poetry, with all this done in prayer, with plenty of laughter to boost our spirit.

Holy Thursday evening, we gathered in the chapel as a missionary priest from Ireland journeyed with us through a special Eucharist in which we washed each other's feet. A holy and profound Good Friday brought us to a reenactment of Jesus' journey to his death. Each sister wrote her own script as she dramatized a Station of the Cross. Unbelievable creativity and deep emotion filled our little meeting room. After a reverencing of the Cross by all, Sister Kandy, Provincial of the Comboni Sisters, led us in a ritual of breaking bread. We processed out into the courtyard where the Cross was positioned in the ground.

On Holy Saturday evening we attended Liturgy that lasted for four hours. The African people and the missionaries to Africa really know how to enhance the rituals of Holy Saturday. More than sixty people were baptized and annointed, as those assembled sang songs, clapped, drummed, danced and celebrated their relatives and friends being baptized and confirmed. We prayed for all of this while sitting on wooden benches with no backs. More than a thousand people attended the service, filling the church, with many standing outside on the dusty road. The line to receive Jesus in the Eucharist at communion seemed to have no end.

It was after one o'clock in the morning by the time we got back to the Comboni Sisters' home. To our surprise, the table was set for a feast when we walked in the door. Afterwards we crawled into our beds, with a few mosquitoes to greet us.

Easter Sunday, Sister Kandy drove us to her former parish for Mass. Other cushion free wooded planks served us as we processed through all the ups and downs the rituals require. The Mass included five weddings and thirty plus baptisms of babies and young children, that included eight processions down the middle aisle and around a side aisle for each part of the baptism ritual.

After the Mass, Sister Kandy drove us home through the impoverished areas in which she worked for eight years. At one place, she stopped to greet Andrew, a child she had come to know while working there. He had no shoes. She got out of the car and measured his foot using a piece of cardboard found near the road and promised him a pair of shoes when she returned.

We noticed there were multiple children just like Andrew who would not be able to receive the shoes they needed. We became aware of the tears in our eyes and the throbs of our hearts in experiencing how God's people have to live, as we saw thousands of children who would not receive the basic necessities of a healthy life.

Easter Sunday afternoon, Sister Lali and Sister Anns took us to a market, where hundreds of vendors gather every Sunday to sell their wares in order to keep from starving. Some gifts for family found at the market would take the spirit of Africa back home upon our return.

Easter Monday is a holiday in Lusaka. To celebrate, we gathered for a delicious barbecue under one of the many trees in the Comboni Sisters' courtyard. Unbeknown to us, there were what seemed millions of ants underfoot. It was only a few seconds before we realized ants were coming out of every aperture of our clothing, and it took only one second to respond to the Sisters' call to get our feet off the ground and onto the rung of the chairs. Whew! We must admit we were still shaking ants from us without letting the sisters become aware of it. We were getting pretty good at faking our lack of distress, when screams were right at the tip of our tongue.

After the barbecue, we piled into a pickup truck, with five of the sisters riding on chairs and mats in the back of the pickup and six of us riding in the cab. This must have been a sight for inquisitive eyes. There are no traffic laws in Zambia to break regarding how many may ride in a truck.

Our purpose was to see African animals in a special park where the animals run free, except lions and elephants, which are fenced. We walked the pathways for several miles, ready to behold animals coming into view. To our chagrin, we saw only a big bird, an African

Eagle which symbolizes freedom and is depicted on the Zambian flag. We saw it in a pasture before entering the park and one deer at a distance as we were leaving.

We had lots of laughs over all the animals we did not see at the animal park. We also had lots of laughs trying to pronounce various words in five launguages represented in the cab of the pickup. We were getting petty good at rolling the r-sound to please our Italian Sisters.

At 4 p.m. that afternoon, the Franciscan Sisters of Assisi arrived to take us to Luansha to give the second retreat of our trip to them. Upon arriving at our retreat destination, we were each provided with a bedroom and bath with a shower. However, one of us had to grow accustomed to accepting a sizable spider, we named Charlotte, that stood watch and protected from mosquitoes. The other had to contend with a grasshopper that carried in a huge beetle for its breakfast, which caused a rumpus on the first sighting.

The Franciscan Missionary Sisters who would participate in the Wholeness/Holiness Retreat began arriving from bush territories throughout Zambia. There was an instant spiritual connection as stories of their ministries began pouring forth, unbelieveable stories of ministering to the poverty-ridden people with little food, huts for homes which are flooded during the rainy season, illnesses with little medical service provided, education for children only a dream as they long for donors who will assist them by providing for this dire need, isolation with little electricity to enable communication with phones and computers, conveniences that we take for granted.

To our amazement, the sisters who live in Zambia on a daily basis do not stress the poverty. Their focus is on ways to relieve the people's poverty. Hope is their theme. Their faces would glow when relating how they built a home for a family who slept standing up in the corner of their hut to keep from sleeping in the water for the three-month-long rainy season. Then there are those who serve in a small hospital without a supply of water for four days or who provide small plots of land in teaching the people how to plant and raise their food, putting familes to work in the western province of Mongu, making nutritional powder and a Vaseline-like ointment from the leaves of plants. Then there are the sisters who find families to take in orphans who stand crying at their doors. It is humbling that we would have anything to give spirtually and holistically to this population of God's chosen ones who do Beatitude living.

The Wholeness/Holiness Retreat experience plunges us to the depth of encounter where divine-human energy collides into oneness. When that happens, a Pentecost explosion abounds in unprepared moments within the gathered retreatants. Songs burst forth, proclamations are shouted out. There are times of silence so deep that even breathing is inaudible, listening so intently that a soul picture is taken and then shown back to the speaker who then feels caught and embraced.

Distance from each other is breached in a new found intimacy. Tears are dried and fatigue dissolves in the embrace of their sisters. And then there are moments when the African spirit rocks the upper room in heart-rendering songs voiced, sung, drummed, trilled, and swayed to recorded music donated by the composers, as well as their own local melodies.

Life is lived by the sisters in Zambia within the Spirit, in one giant circular motion of life, death and life. How humbling it is to be gathered in this upper room, where all divisions fade away and Jesus' words of oneness resound. When this happens, we dive deeply into the mystery of all being one in the world we know and in the universe yet to be known. All we can say is "Wow!", a word which is used and taught to the African children to express experiences of wonder in doing something well.

At the finish of the retreat we said our farewells and blessings as the sisters departed to their places of ministry. Their spirit would always live within us and will assist us in going forth to give our third retreat to the Comboni Sisters.

What was symbolized in this retreat and others is how religious communities of women around the world model the authority of Jesus, in which authority is "one with" rather than "one over." The Provincial Teams (Leadership Teams) made the retreat along with the sisters whom they serve. Upon leaving this retreat, the Provincial said to one of her sisters, "I am at your service."

Our third retreat found us back with the Comboni Sisters near Lusaka. Attending were six Comboni Sisters and two Sisters of the Incarnate Word from San Antonio, Texas, who were missioned to Mongu, a nine-hour drive by bus to Lusaka. Despite the colds being passed from one to the other, we managed to dive deep and surface with renewed energy and dedication to the poor being served so magnanimously by all the sisters.

Immediately following the retreat, we embarked on a seven-hour unbelievable happening with Sister Josephine and Sister Rita. Two years prior, Sister Josephine spent a week at Mount St. Francis upon completion of her knee surgery in Wisconsin, which was arranged by Sister Connie Fahey.

Our first venture of the morning was to a small immigration office near the Zambian copper mines to extend our visas for an additional three weeks. Sister Josephine's driver took us to a small unofficious office, empty except for three immigration officers who greeted us with broad smiles, inviting us to come right in. Upon learning the length of time we were requesting, they unquestioningly stamped our visas for an additional month and invited us to come back again for a third month. The ease of this procedure was a welcomed surprise. We had expected at least some difficulty with extending our tourist visas.

The Franciscan Missionary Sisters of Assisi have been and are accomplishing miracles for the poorest area we have ever, ever seen. They have set up a food distribution center for around thirty children who are literally starving. The food is prepared by volunteer mothers who give homes and feed the childern. They receive guidance in meal planning and preparation by a nutritionist. There is a government school just across the road, so the children come from school to the feeding center every day. There is land to plant maize to be used for the feeding program.

Next, Sister Josephine took us to an area where we met children and mothers who live in unimaginable poverty. They are in an area smaller than a city block. More than four hundred mothers and children were living in homes put together with cardboard boxes and grass roofs, providing the barest protection from weather or whatever.

Waiting for adoption procedures to take place, one of the mothers was keeping an orphan infant on nothing but a thin blanket covered with dirt. It took us several minutes to take in the sight, as the shock waves of this atrocity caused our hearts to almost stop beating. It was a paralysis moment as we took in utter human depravement of women and children in our human family. Men were depicted only by the reality of many of the women pregnant.

The children seemed fascinated by our white skin and were eager just to touch it. Even in this dire poverty, the children led us in an African rhythm of hands clapping and bodies moving to musical sounds that seemed to come from their very souls. A tiny one-year-old girl took center stage in leading those gathered.

During the next two hours, we were on a whirlwind tour, experiencing life on the Zambian-Congo border, then spending time at two plots of land donated to the Franciscan Missionary Sisters of Assisi and meeting the family working the land with crops of maize and sweet potatoes. Children were everywhere and again the poverty reached our hearts. No schools were in sight for miles, which means that most of the children we saw would not be getting an education.

We could not wrap our minds around the numbers of children, who seemed to come from everywhere in every place, peeking out from around every bush, with one group poorer than another and with so little available in education, health care, transportation, clean water and nutrition. We were told that if a growing girl does not have a child of her own, she is considered unsatisfactory by her family and even the African society.

It is beyond our capacity to address, which leaves us haunted by the reality. We are so proud of the religious communities of Sisters of Zambia, who are giving of their health, time, energy, and their very lives to make a difference. International collaboration is the only way that would be large enough to make a dent in lifting the impoverishment of the people. It is incredible to think that this situation is mulitiplied many times over in a myriad of countries throughout the world.

We had been invited to Solwezi by Bishop Charles Kasonde. He called us to say that he had been at a Bishops' meeting in Lusaka and while there he was diagnosed with malaria plus infection. However, he was sending Father Chola, the Vicar of the Diocese of Solwezi, to drive us to Solwezi. This would be a three-hour ride on mostly unpaved and unbelievably potholed roadways.

When we arrived, Sister Norma, of the Mercedarian Missionaries of Berriz, had our itinerary all planned. A highlight was meeting thirty children who are being educated through donations from the United States, a direct benefit of the connection now established between our two countries! As the need in Zambia has been shared, hearts have been moved and resources for meeting the need have been tapped. Some of the donors contribute from their abundance, while others share from their limited allowances. It takes all of us to lift families out of poverty wherever possible.

Even though the students were on holiday, they dressed up in their uniforms and came to meet us. They talked with us about their future goals and expressed multiple thanks to all the donors from

America who are responsible for their receiving an education. All the children were those who would not be receiving an education without financial help. One of the children, a sixteen year-old boy

named Derick, had been asked by his mother at age thirteen to leave home and find his own way in life, because she could no longer house and feed him along with all her other children.

Another highlight was visiting a fresh water well, made possible by donors, that was drilled for an impoverished community in Mitakutuku. Since drilling the well, the community is able to grind their maize, rebuild a small church, and increase health for the whole community. It is a miracle what water can do.

The third highlight brought us to St. Francis Mission, operated by the Baptiste Missionary Sisters. The work of these sisters educates women for basic survival and living skills. Because of travel distance, they provide room and board for women who attend classes. They also board junior high school girls, who live there during the week and cook their own food and care for themselves and each other.

One sister operates a clinic, offering a range of services from delivering babies, to running laboratory tests, to treating malaria and prescribing medication. Because of the great distances they have to walk, mothers and unborn babies often die before they arrive at the clinic.

The reality of leprosy was brought into our consciousness as we interacted with God's special ones who are maimed or crippled in multiple ways by the devastating disease. Time spent with lepers and their families who live adjacent to the clinic will be permanently etched into the depths of our being.

The isolation and exclusion from human touch and

disfigurement of the leper brought us to reach out and touch and converse with a man who yearned to engage with us. Is any entity working to eliminate this atrocious disease, which will no longer be a figment of our imagination? How long will it take for medical research and treatment to reach those who live in desperation?

Drawn by a leper at the edge of the colony, Margie walked over and knelt to meet his gaze and touch his shoulder. She spent ten minutes listening and communing in Spirit. The words spoken were lost in the absence of translation, but the spirits given and received were understood, welcomed and celebrated.

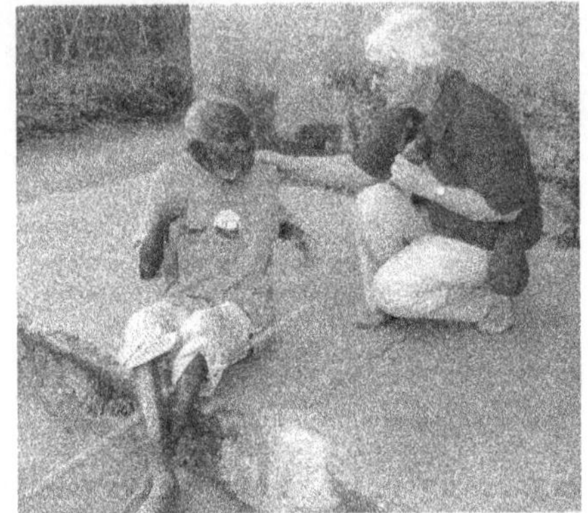

Going to and from the mission, we traversed the worst bush trail, unimaginable without seeing it. Returning from the mission, we got stuck in a mound of mud just before a waterhole. Even with the four-wheel drive and four on the floor transmission, we had a tinge of fear that darkness would settle before we could move. Some young men wanted kwacha (money) before helping us. Father Roy got out of the vehicle and maneuvered some rocks in order to back out of the hole. This enabled us to spin our way over the mud and through the waterhole on our way out.

The following morning, Bishop Charles Kasonde drove us to an airstrip where we were delighted to board a small plane to take us to Lusaka, quite a step up from traveling the potholed roads by car.

We are familied into the Love of our God so that we can exist into loving all that is, wherever we happen to find ourselves. In the words of Sister Ilia Delio, in *The Unbearable Wholeness of*

Being, "Love is the unifier, it brings us together, it is ever creative, it is energy upon energy towards oneness."We are encountering the truth of her statement from the same source, "Tribalism opposes evolution when the boundaries of separateness resist the urge to unify."

As Mystic Julian of Norwich put it, "By myself I am nothing at all, but in general, I am in the oneing of love, for it is this oneing that the life of all people exists." Continuing, "In the sight of God, all humans are oned, and one person is all people and all people are one person."

We need a birthquake, one that will bend our minds, warm our hearts, increase our dreams, and expand our horizons. Our final prayer is from the book, "*The Writings of St. Clare,*"

What you hold, may you (always) hold,
What you do, may you (always) do and never abandon
But with swift pace, light step,
unswerving feet,
so that even your steps stir up no dust,
may you go forward
securely, joyfully, and swiftly,
on the path of prudent happiness,
not believing anything,
not agreeing with anything
that would dissuade you from this resolution
or that would place a stumbling block for you
on the way,
so that you may offer your vows to the Most High
in the pursuit of that perfection

SISTER MARGIE HOSCH, OSF, SISTER CONNIE FAHEY, FSM,
MARY CATHERINE HARRIS, BILL HANCOCK

to which the Spirit of the Lord has called you.

On the sixth trip, Sister Margie and Mary Catherine gave three Wholeness/Holiness Retreats.

Letter fron Office of Bishop Kasonde, Solwezi, Zambia:

A Living Legacy Of Two American Catholic
Sisters Who Touched A Zambian Diocese

Sr. Krista Namio, a Mercedarian Sister working in the office of the Bishop of the Catholic Diocese Solwezi as Secretary, had an unforgettable experience of her retreat in Lusaka, Zambia's capital city. The retreat was facilitated by Sr. Connie and Sr. Margie. Sr. Krista was profoundly touched by the presentation of these two American Sisters and the content of the retreat they facilitated. That experience made her want other Sisters from Solwezi Diocese to experience the same. She was instrumental in bringing Srs. Connie and Margie to Solwezi. The Local Ordinary, Bishop Charles J. S. Kasonde did not hesitate to extend an invitation and quickly facilitated the sisters' visit to his diocese.

In July 2011, the two sisters returned to Zambia for another tour to give retreats to religious Sisters in Lusaka. Prior arrangements had been made that the two sisters visit Solwezi Diocese to direct retreats for all the religious Men, Women and Clergy of the diocese, after the Lusaka mission.

As planned, Srs. Connie and Margie came. The retreats were overwhelmingly attended. Two retreats were held: one for religious sisters and the other for religious men and priests serving the Catholic Diocese of Solwezi at the time. In terms of numbers, approximately 60 religious and priests were in attendance!

The religious and clergy were more than appreciative with what they had gained during their particular retreat gatherings. The general feedback solicited indicated that nearly everyone was looking forward to having another retreat with them the following year.

Srs. Connie and Margie became very well known and endeared to all the Religious and Priests of the diocese. Everyone remained with the hope that someday they would return to conduct the retreats. It was evident that the retreats had so re-energized us in spirit and strength that we were filled with hope and motivation to continue our challenging mission in the vineyard of God in this part of the world.

One would ask why these spiritual gatherings conducted by Srs. Connie and Margie proved popular. There was a sense of ease, simplicity and depth of spiritual awareness that characterised the retreats. They were so well organized by two sisters that there was almost a melodious symphony to them. The coordination between the two when conducting the retreats had a novelty and freshness that was attractive as it was captivating!

Before leaving for Lusaka, Bishop Kasonde personally conducted a tour for Connie and Margie. They visited the Diocesan Curia and some spots within Solwezi town to get familiar with some of the pastoral activities the Diocese was undertaking. The tour was limited due to lack of time. They did not see much but they were touched.

The following year, the American sisters were back again in Lusaka doing what they knew best, conducting retreats and extending their hand of charity where they saw fit. As a diocese, we were lucky, too. In spite of the rough terrain getting here, they came. This time, they wanted to tour the diocese a little further than Solwezi town. They were taken to see the Rural Health Centres of St. Francis Mission located 50Km from Solwezi and Mumbzhi's Holy Family 120Km from Solwezi.

Defying age and relying on their youthful hearts, the two sisters joined Bishop Kasonde on his normally taxing Episcopal Pastoral visits to the parishes and outstations nearby. It is on those visits that they were introduced to our programs of education for the Orphans and Vulnerable Children (OVCs). This experience accorded them the opportunity to witness the real situation of the lives of OVCs. It is this exposure to the challenges of our pastoral situation that undoubtedly made huge impressions on them. They went back to the USA fully mindful of these experiences and the many uncountable stories to tell.

Since then they have become very instrumental in providing the much needed finances to help in the running of some of the pastoral programs of the Diocese. Needless to mention, the sisters have been providing funds every year and making a contribution towards fuel for Bishop Charles Kasonde's visits to the remotest parishes in the Diocese.

It must be noted here that the distance between the two furthest parishes is almost 600Km! The road network is generally in a very deplorable state. There has been an inflow of funds for the Orphans and Vulnerable Children. These funds, under the auspices of Sr. Connie and Sr. Margie, have been used to take children back to school. With their assistance, we have been providing funds for a sewing Project for women as well as giving funds for women to kick-start their income generating projects. They also provided funds for four (4) boreholes to parishes and outstations. One borehole was dug for one of the Religious Sister's Congregation. Without doubt, clean and safe water is of utmost importance for the health of our people. Aside from money, they also send us boxes of books for Religious Sisters, Clergy and for the children; boxes of clothing, rosaries and toiletries. To alleviate a shortfall of paraphernalia in hospitals, they managed to send us a huge container filled with hospital beds, wheel chairs, weighing scales, gloves, chairs and all sorts of medical equipment and medicines. It was a very big help not only for the St. Francis and Holy Family rural health centres but also the other 3 health centres that are further than the two that they had earlier visited.

The Diocese of Solwezi is one of the poorest in Zambia. It was our hope that the coming of mining companies to Solwezi would help us to be self-sustainable. However, most of those who are employed in the mines are drawn from other provinces and are not permanently residents of Sowezi. As a way of trying to generate finances for the local Church, The Diocesan Management, spearheaded by His Lordship Charles Kasonde, put together a team of professional and committed Catholics to form the Diocesan Investment Portfolio. However, we still have a long way to go to attain our goal to adequately accomplish our mission of "Integral Evangelization of God's People." The Diocese is still heavily dependent on outside assistance, both financial and material, to run its pastoral (and social) programs.

It is gladdening and heart-warming to note that the sacrifice and charitable works of Sister Connie and Sister Margie are helping us in a huge way to venture and implement our pastoral initiatives and reach out to the poorest of the poor in the Diocese of Solwezi.

We are indeed blessed to have Sister Connie and Sister Margie as our partners in working in the vineyard of the Lord and we remain mightily grateful to God for their vocation to the Church and donation of their lives. It is through their love, prayers, financial and material support, that we are progressing in the mission of "Integral Evangelization of God's People."

We are bereft of words to thank them enough for what they have done and continue to do. All we know is that God will reward them for all that they are doing to the least of our brothers and sisters in this world, particularly those whose lives they touch in the Catholic Diocese of Solwezi.

Compiled By

Fr. Neal Mulyata	Sr. Norma Atilano, MMB
Vicar General	Projects Secretary

EPILOGUE

When a spark ignites a choice from what is deepest and highest within, there is a Trasna moment. It may tap one's profound desire beneath the more shallow, or mark a spot of unexpected connection between seeking and finding. Recognition of need in another may give rise to compassion that promps a personal response. One person's call may inspire support from an entire community. The potential seems infinite for Trasna moments.

Such moments abound within the hearts and experiences of these reflections on coming to know part of our human family in Zambia. Within a multitude of individuals and communities, the choices for the greater good have been agents of "multiplying the loaves and fish to feed the masses." The movement of Spirit between one giver and one receiver in a retreat experience some years ago served as the first morsel for the feeding that continues to this day in mutual giving and receiving.

Multiplication has expanded the mission beyond the initial vision and visionaries. Spirits have been enlivened. Provisions have visibly enabled life. These continue to sustain and give hope for life for some of the most impoverished in our human family.

Among the provisions are fresh water wells, medical supplies, education and library supplies, school tuition, shoes and clothing for children and adults, transportation, support for Zambian enterprise, and retreats and spiritual companionship. Behind the scenes have been fund-raisers, sewing circles, shipping underwriting and prayer and more prayer. Dreams for the future are yet in formation. There is no period on either the need or the commitment and support, as the travelers continue to walk and talk and give and receive.

Some in the journey have given from their abundance, others in their poverty. Some have been visible, others in the background. The intended receivers have graciously offered hospitality of place and self. Along the way, the giving and receiving have become intermingled in one joyous cycle.

So, it is with deep gratitude that we acknowledge the donors and recipients, our fellow travelers, who are too numerous and universal to name, who are now a part of the journey and continuing mission in Zambia. We appreciate each giver and gift. Although we cannot identify one by one, the names are etched within those whose lives have been enriched. We celebrate with each person and community the Trasna moment which may have prompted the first step onto the pathway and all steps to follow. We celebrate the Spirit which stirs us and draws us together in companionship and compassion with one another.

We are grateful for the generosity of Bill Hancock, the author, and Bob O'Brien of Prose Press, the publisher, who offer themselves as conveyors of the story, that others may be invited into the journey. As we go forward, may we desire the grace of openness, and trust ourselves to the leading of each spark and star that rises deep within. May we know there will be light for our steps and may we offer ourselves to be the light.

Sister Margie Hosch, OSF
Sister Connie Fahey, FSM
Mary Catherine Harris

Sources Material For this Book

Material from Sister Margie Hosch, OSF:

- E-mail Sept 8, 2017 - What was I feeling and thinking on the first flight to Zambia
- E-mail Sept 12, 2017 – My parents
- E-mail Sept 18, 2017 - Dancing
- E-mail Sept 20, 2017 – Experience of growing up in the Hosch family
- A "Sigh" Without End – 2009
- Taking Flight - 2010
- Designed to Fly – 2010
- "Have a banana. Have two bananas!" - July, 2011
- Jesus Prayer to You – Love large, O my people! (Provided to Zambian Religious)
- BURSTING BREATH – 2012
- A Report to Our Donors – 2013
- Bonded by Being - 2013
- ALLELUIA! ALLELUIA! ALLELUIA! - 2014
- EASTER WEEK – 2014
- DEEPENING OUR CAPACITY TO LOVE – 2014
- SO LATE HAVE I LOVED YOU – 2014

Material from Sister Connie Fahey, FSM:

- Hearing the Cry of the Poor
- My Thirty Day Retreat, Zambia – 2009
- Reflections on My Second Trip to Africa – 2010
- Was it a Vision or a Flashback? - 2010

- Dear Friends and Family – July, 2011
- Do They Know How Beautiful They Are? - 2012
- TO DIE TO GIVE LIFE -2013
- Bonded by Being - 2013

Material from Mary Catherine Harris:

- Coming to Know Sister Margie Hosch – 2010
- E-mail Sept 11, 2017 – Introduction to Sr. Margie Hosch
- HOPE YOU'RE SITTING DOWN BUT CAN YOU FLY? - 2014
- LETTING GO – 2014
- E-mails Sept 14 & 15, 2017 - Bits and Pieces

Other Material Sources:

- Sister Raphael Cortsdine, PBVM – Poem (Published by PBVM in *Songs for the Journey)*
- St. John Vianney Parish, Janesville, WI Flyer – Lenten Service Project
- 2007 Flyer about Sister Margie Hosch when she left Catholic Charities in Greenville, SC
- E-mails and phone exchanges, not already listed, between Sept, 2017 and Date of Publication
- Pictures provided by the co-authors of this book

CPSIA information can be obtained
at www.ICGtesting.com
Printed in the USA
FSHW04n0959110418
46582FS